To: Toni,

May you receive healing and deliverance as you journey through the pages of my story! Remember you are enough and you deserve the the best! Jesus paid it all for you with His Blood and you are his Royal daughter!

From: Ms. Tonya

from
BLOODSTAINS
-to the -
BLOOD-STAINED
BANNER

PASTOR TANYA PRICE

FROM BLOODSTAINS
TO THE
BLOOD-STAINED
BANNER

Pastor Tanya Price

FROM BLOODSTAINS
TO THE BLOOD-STAINED BANNER

The Blood-Stained Banner is the Emblem of Victory!

Tanya Arnette Price
Precise Christian Ministries
P.O. Box 9579
Ontario, California 91762
precise.christianministries@yahoo.com
(909)414-5401

Copyright © August 2022
ISBN: 978-1-7358211-7-7

For additional information, please contact:
(909) 414-5401

For information about special discounts for bulk purchases please contact the Special Sales Department at sew2direct@yahoo.com

Library of Congress Cataloging-in Publication Data
Tanya Price

Published by Executive Business Writing
P.O. Box 10002,
Moreno Valley, CA 92552
(951)488-7634
https://www.beverlycrockett.com
executivebusinesswriting@gmail.com

Edited by Julie Boney
JB Editing Solutions
www.jb-editingsolutions.com

Graphics by Tracy Spencer
Legacy Media, LLC
Moreno Valley, CA 92552

TABLE OF CONTENTS

FOREWORD

From Bloodstains to the Blood-Stained Banner by Pastor Tanya Price is a riveting testimony of the power of the blood that still speaks of our deliverance and such a great salvation! (1 John 5:8). This book is very needed today for the born-again as well as the unsaved because in the body of Christ we are sometimes ashamed of what Jesus has already brought us through. Our testimony is an encouragement to the unsaved of what the saving power of the blood of Jesus can bring them out of, such as shame, guilt, fear, and self-destruction. God has given us a new start (new life) in Christ!

I have known Pastor Tanya for over 15 years and have worked alongside her in ministry. The truth of her life is an example of what each of us can overcome through the blood of Jesus Christ — complete victory in every area of our lives. The standing and staying power of the blood has already healed, restored, delivered, and cleansed us from and through any situation.

Through this book about the word of our testimony, and the blood-stained banner, we receive freedom in our families, marriages, sons, daughters, friends, etc. In this book, Tanya offers God's solution to our afflictions. From the abundance of her heart and experience, she shares real solutions to loss, identity confusion, broken relationships, and emotional dysfunction. I know you will be healed and restored in your heart, and find your identity and forgiveness, and the cleansing power of the blood.

Yes, let's continue to honor the blood of Jesus Christ. *"For we overcome by the blood of the Lamb and the word of our testimony"* (Rev. 12:11). I commend Tanya Price for accepting this divine assignment, which I know will have a life-altering effect on individuals and families for generations to come.

Pastor Janice Huizar
Woman of Divine Destiny

ACKNOWLEDGEMENTS

I want to first give all glory and honor to my Lord and Savior Jesus Christ. Without Him I would be lost. He rescued me from the pit of destruction. Jesus showed me what true love is, and I don't take it lightly that He has entrusted me with the gospel of His holy name. I thank Him for allowing me to minister healing, deliverance, hope, and encouragement through this book. May God get all the glory, for without the ultimate sacrifice of His blood, I wouldn't have made it through to tell my story.

I would also like to thank my wonderful God-fearing husband for being patient with me, giving me the time and space while I worked on this project. I couldn't have asked for a better loving, giving, and supportive husband, who believes in me and always encourages me that there is more for me in God. I also would like to thank him for loving and caring for my sons as his own, and living a Godly example of integrity before them.

I would like to thank my sons for their love, forgiveness, and patience while God was working on me to bring healing and deliverance to me and our family. I thank you for your courage in allowing me to tell our story.

I also must acknowledge my dad, the late Carl Brodie, Sr., Ph.D., for encouraging me to write this book and giving me tools to accomplish it. Also, Hattie and Robert Yancy, for being like parents to me. Hattie, God sent me to you because He knew you would nurture and care for me and fill my void of not having a mother. Thank you for being there for me and your grandchildren in our most difficult times, always pouring in wisdom and knowledge.

I would like to thank Liz Pereda, with Project I Am, for the training and mentoring she provided for writing my book. I didn't know where to start, but your training program was very easy to follow. Thank you for your encouragement!

Finally, I would like to thank Dr. Beverly Crockett-Goudy for utilizing her God-given gifts and talents that the Lord has given her. Thank you for walking in excellence, integrity, and professionalism with Executive Business Writing. God couldn't have connected me with and entrusted this project to a better person to edit and publish this book. I am grateful for the spirit of God in you!

Tanya Price

Pastor, Precise Christian Ministries

INTRODUCTION

As a young girl, I realized there are many things that are out of our control. Your parents make decisions for you that can either make or break you, and then you end up repeating the cycle if that cycle is not broken. Because of some of these choices, I was stripped of my innocence and identity, and my voice was taken from me. All that was left were insecurities, low self-esteem, and lack of confidence.

I was aware, at a young age, of God's love and protection that I later would see was the only thing that carried me through. God had a plan for my life that no devil in hell could stop. I felt very strongly in my spirit that I must tell my story to let people see the victories, the struggles, the hardships, the failures, and the triumph, and that after the storm, the sun will shine through!

I experienced a lot of pain and trauma, as you will find out while reading my story. You might even be reminded of your own pain, trauma, failures, struggles, and regrets. The good news is that the same God who brought me through to victory by the power of His blood will also bring you through.

As I was writing this book, I had to come face to face with the events in my past — those wounds that were buried deep down inside of me. I realized that although I experienced some healing and deliverance, some of my wounds were not completely healed. There are parts of my story that I am not proud of, that I did not want to talk about, but I knew that I had to be totally transparent, real, and raw in order for others to be healed and set free. I could not let the devil take me back to a place of shame and guilt that God had already freed me from so that I could help somebody else get to the other side of their trauma.

Sometimes you feel like you are alone, and no one can relate to your story, and the devil keeps you bound with shame and guilt, not wanting you to experience the love and forgiveness of our heavenly Father. What you keep hidden doesn't get healed. The devil works in the dark. The devil tries to keep us blind to our identity in Christ, therefore keeping us ignorant of our authority we have in His name and in the power of the blood. My prayer is that through this book you will come to know your identity in Christ and the power He has given you to take authority over the devil. Through the power of the blood-stained banner, you too will overcome by the blood of the Lamb and the word of your testimony (Revelation 12:11).

My scars are now a reminder of an all-powerful God who is able to go down into our heart and soul and reach the depths of our hurt and pain, and pull it up from the root and bring the complete healing that we need to walk fully in our purpose and destiny. I believe that your life will be undoubtfully impacted by walking through this journey with me to your healing and deliverance. It's time for your healing. Let the healing begin!

Introduction

Chapter 1

MY FIRST HEARTBREAK

My heart sank to my stomach, and I had a lump in my throat as I tried to fight back the tears. You see, just moments earlier I was so excited because my mom said if I hurried up to take my bath I could stay up for a little while to draw and color before bed. Drawing and coloring were my favorite things to do at 5 years old because it took me out of the present chaos in my world, and it took me to a place where I could dream that my world was perfect. I would draw pictures of my world that were peaceful and beautiful. I colored my world with lots of flowers, trees, and bright colors instead of darkness. I drew a family that was always smiling together and happy all the time.

Just as I started to draw, my brother started teasing me about my picture. "Your picture is ugly; you can't draw!" "My picture is not ugly." "Yes, it is," he said. I began to cry as I yelled, "No it's not. Mom, can you make Morie stop teasing me? He said my picture is ugly and that I can't draw."

The teasing and ridicule happened on a continual basis, and that was the beginning of my self-esteem and confidence being torn down. I felt like I couldn't do anything well enough. My brother was always picking on me, criticizing me, and teasing me.

I was raised in a family with five sisters and one brother, so you can only imagine how loud our home was. It had some joy and laughter, as well as lots of teasing, fighting, screaming, and competition amongst us siblings.

My father and mother always had their friends and neighbors over, and loved to drink, play music, and have card games. When I was 5 years old my world came crashing down. I was told that my mother and father were getting a divorce. I didn't know quite what that all meant at 5 years old, but I soon realized, after my dad moved my mom and us children out of our home in La Puente, California, to a city called Pacoima in the San Fernando Valley, that it meant we would no longer be a family and my dad and mom would no longer be together.

In our home in Pacoima, I had an awareness that God was with me. God would warn me in dreams of things to come so I would be aware of danger and of good things to come. I didn't know it then, but I had the gift of prophecy and seeing visions. My first dream came at 5 years old. In my dream, a stranger knocked on my mom's door, and when I said, "Who is there?" he said, "It's daddy." But when I looked out the curtain, it really was a stranger. The next day I was expecting my dad to pick us up for our weekend visit. There was a knock on the door, and I ran to the door, excited to see my dad. I said, "Who is it?" and he said, "It's daddy; open the door." I immediately remembered the dream I had the night before. I looked out the curtain and sure enough, it was a stranger! Frightened, I ran to tell my mom. This only made my mom even more fearful. Since my dad had divorced my mom, she was dealing with rejection, abandonment, depression, anxiety, and fear.

Shortly after this, I remember feeling sad and confused, especially when my dad would pick us up for the weekends and take us to his new home, which, by the way, was around the corner from our old family home in La Puente. I was also very hurt and confused to find out that our neighbor who lived across the street from our family home was now my dad's new wife and my stepmother.

I don't know how I knew it at such a young age, but somehow, I knew this was the reason my dad and mom had divorced. I noticed my mom started being really scared all the time in our new home, which I had never seen before in our other family home. I would awaken to my mom screaming in the middle of the night, saying that there was a man on the roof or a man in the closet.

My mom became very unstable and was always frightened. I remember hearing my brother, who was 8 years older than me at the time, saying that my dad hired people to drive my mom crazy so he could prove her mentally unstable to gain full custody of us children. You see, I was born in the 60's, when it was very rare for the father to get custody of the children. It almost always went to the mother. However, my father succeeded, and my mother went into a mental institution and later into a group home for adults who had mental illnesses. Those were some of the hardest times for me, visiting my mom in those mental homes, seeing the state of her mind. I didn't know it then, but when I was a teenager, I started declaring over my life that I will never let a man drive me crazy. It ended up that my dad was given full custody of us.

My sister, who was 10 years older than me, started rebelling when she was in the 6th grade. She started running away from home, hanging out with older guys, and getting into trouble stealing cars, and landed herself in juvenile hall, and later in and out of prison.

I always had a lot of compassion for my sister when we would go visit her in jail. I always cried when we had to leave her there when our visit was over. Another sister would always elbow me in the back seat of the car on the way home and tell me to stop being so emotional. I didn't know it then, but God was giving me a heart for prisoners. Later in life, when I gave my life to the Lord, I ended up in prison ministry, volunteering in the juvenile halls and camps, conducting church services. That came back full circle. God begins to stir those gifts up in you early in life before you even know your calling.

I remember being very quiet as a child, frightened, insecure, and shy. As I got older, our visits with our mom became fewer and fewer. I was always sad, and longed for my mother. God put in us the desire to seek a mother's nurturing and loving care. This placed a huge void in my heart, which left me very vulnerable. My dad had stopped taking us to see our mom, so two of my older sisters would take my younger sister and me on the bus to see her.

Now mind you, they were only 13 and 11 years old at the time. My younger sister was 5 and I was 8 years old. We lived in La Puente, California, and our mom lived in Long Beach, California, which is about 31 miles away. We had to take three buses to get to Long Beach, and my sisters were just kids themselves, who really didn't have the bus system figured out.

We were not prepared for the traumatic experience we were about to encounter. All we knew was we longed to see our mother. We left the house late one afternoon. The day was warm, and we were dressed for the weather. My sisters thought we would arrive before nightfall, but the buses didn't connect us on time to transfer to our last bus and we ended up in downtown Los Angeles at 10pm. We missed the last bus going into Long Beach for the night. The next bus would not come until 5am the following day.

I was terrified, cold, and hungry. We cuddled together under a store front downtown, trying to keep each other safe and warm. This was my first experience with homelessness, drunkards, and people out of their minds, walking the streets at night.

The daybreak couldn't come fast enough. It felt like a lifetime went by. I was so happy to hear the bus coming up the street so that we could finally be safe and warm from the cold and scary streets. We arrived at my mom's safely, and were so overjoyed to see her. When it was time to take the trip back home, I was so sad, and the tears began to fall from my eyes. I didn't want to leave my mom and I was also frightened of taking the bus trip back through the streets of downtown Los Angeles. You can only imagine how this traumatized me and only added to my being shy and insecure.

If your childhood was anything like mine, you can relate to my story. Have you ever just felt empty, frightened, lost, and alone, and felt like you just weren't good enough? You see, God showed me He was there for me from the beginning. He had His arms of protection covering me, and He is there for you right now.

God tells us in Jeremiah 1:5, *"Before I formed you in the womb I knew you; before you were born, I set you apart; I appointed you as a prophet to the nations."* I would look up in the sky with my eyes full of tears and my heart feeling like it was in a million pieces; yet somehow knowing that God would see my tears, heartache, loneliness, and emptiness. You can find comfort in knowing He is the God that sees. He sees you just like He sees me. He knows your heart is broken. He sees your tears and emptiness.

Genesis 16:13, *"She (Hagar) gave this name to the LORD who spoke to her: 'You are the God who sees me,' for she said, 'I have now seen the One who sees me."* We read in Psalm 56:8, *"You keep track of all my sorrows. You have collected all my tears in your bottle. You have recorded each one in Your book."*

The good news is that He doesn't leave us in that condition, for the same God who sees is also the God who heals. Psalm 147:3 says, *"He heals the brokenhearted, and binds up their wounds."*

My First Heartbreak

Chapter 2

PAIN UNDER THE SHEETS

Saturday morning had finally come. That meant no school and I could wake up early, eat my favorite cereal, Captain Crunch, watch cartoons, and go outside to play with my friends. My day started off like a normal day and ended up a nightmare. My dad told my younger sister and me that his friend was going to pick us up for a couple of hours and take us to his house. I was 6 years old at the time and my sister was 3 years old.

I remember feeling nervous and shy on the car ride to his home as he tried to make small talk with my sister and me. We arrived at his house and until this day I can vividly remember the room. When you enter his home, you walk into the kitchen, which leads into the bedroom and bathroom. It was a little studio apartment. I remember the bathroom didn't have a door on it. There was a sheet in place of it, which I thought was strange. He told my sister and me to take a nap. I was told to go to the bathroom first and leave my panties in the bathroom in case I peed in the bed. I told him I don't pee in the bed, and he said, "Well do it anyway, just in case." I thought to myself that doesn't make sense, but I did what I was told.

My sister and I fell asleep, and I was awakened to pain. My dad's friend, who appeared to be close to 300 pounds, was on top of me, and he was putting his private part in mine. I was crying, saying, "Stop! you're hurting me," and he kept saying, "Shh......don't wake your sister." The more he forced himself into my little body, the more painful it got. I said, "Stop, or I'm telling my daddy; you're hurting me." He said, "No, don't tell. I will buy you ice cream." But I kept saying, "I don't want ice cream. Stop! I'm telling my daddy."

This nightmare seemed like it was never going to end. When he finally stopped, I went to the bathroom and noticed all the blood. I was crying and trembling, and just wanted my daddy. I quickly put my panties on and demanded for him to take me home. I don't think my sister understood what was going on at 3 years old. I cried all the way home as he begged me not to tell my dad and that he would get me ice cream. I kept repeating, "I'm telling my daddy."

When we arrived back home, I was frightened, confused, and afraid. I came into the house and quickly rushed to my room to grab clean panties and my pajamas. My dad must have been in his bedroom, and I hurried to the bathroom to run bath water. I just wanted to wash it all away and forget it ever happened. I took my bloody panties and hid them in the bottom of the trash can. I remember sobbing in the tub and even though I kept threatening to tell my daddy, somehow I thought it was all my fault for listening to the man when he told me to take my panties off. How could I tell my daddy? I thought I would be in trouble; I avoided my dad and went straight to bed. My dad's friend never showed his face again around our house. I remember overhearing my dad saying he moved out of state. I am sure he was afraid I was going to tell on him, and he would be in big trouble.

My world of chaos, insecurity, and pain only got worse. This traumatic experience affected every area of my life. I was introverted and felt like I didn't have a voice. I felt lost, stripped of my innocence, identity, and self-worth. I was frightened and felt so alone. I felt as if all of that man's deviant spirits, such as lust, perversion, and more, were now on me.

I started touching myself and always looking for a place and time to be by myself to masturbate and get aroused. As a teenager I would be interested in older guys and be too afraid to tell them that I didn't want to have sex. So, I would let them take advantage of me.

I became rebellious and didn't want to listen to my dad and became a teenage runaway. I lived a life of a vagabond from age 14 to 18. I was in and out of my father's home, looking for love in all the wrong places. Deep down inside, I blamed my dad for what happened to me that day with his friend. I said to myself, what father in his right mind would let his little girls go with this single man by ourselves to his home. I felt like my daddy, whom I had looked up to, didn't protect me.

Have you ever felt like the very people who were supposed to protect you literally fed you to the wolves? Have you ever blamed yourself for something that was not your fault because you felt like somehow, you caused this to come upon you? Have you ever lived in a world of shame, guilt, and regret? I can relate to these feelings because this was the prison I was trapped in until Jesus came in and told me the truth and canceled the lies of the devil. Hallelujah!

Today I declare that you are coming out too! You can cancel the lies of the devil by speaking these truths over your life. Romans 8:1 declares, *"There is therefore now no condemnation to them which are in Christ Jesus, who walk not after the flesh but the spirit."* God will get the glory out of what you have gone through! Romans 8:28 tells us, *"What the devil meant for evil God will turn it around for the good to those that love him and are called according to His purpose."*

You see, the devil meant to destroy you so that you would not walk into God's call and purpose for your life. John 10:10 reminds us, *"The thief does not come except to steal, and to kill, and destroy. I come that they may have life, and that they may have it more abundantly.*" You are a threat to the devil's kingdom. That's why he tried to take you out early, but you are more than a conqueror through Christ Jesus.

Romans 8:37: "*No, in all these things we are more than conquerors through him who loved us.*" Wow! I see the chains breaking off and the prison walls coming down, in Jesus' name!

Pain Under the Sheets

Chapter 3

YOU ARE NOT FORSAKEN

Nobody ever wants to get that phone call. The one in which the caller is on the other end saying that they are sorry, but there has been an accident.

I was 14 years old when the phone rang and my dad answered it and quickly hung up and said, "Girls, I must tell you something. There was a fire in your mom's apartment. She couldn't get to her wheelchair, and she was burned alive in the fire.

My mother had three strokes before the fire and the last one had left her paralyzed from the waist down. She also didn't know who we were the last time we had seen her; her memory was gone. I remember being so sad when they told her this is your daughter, Tanya, and she just nodded her head. I was so sad that she didn't recognize her own daughter. That would be the last time I would see her alive.

My dad drove us to Long Beach. When we arrived the fire department and crowds of people were in front of the apartment building. I don't know why we were taken there to witness that; I could have done without that memory.

The next day I remember being so sad, looking at all the greeting cards I had bought her and never mailed out. I had so many regrets. My dad entered my room and said it was time to get ready for school. I said, "Dad, I don't want to go to school. I am so sad about mom, and I have a headache from crying all night." My dad said, "I realize you are sad, but you must go to school. Take some Tylenol for your headache and get ready." I thought this was so cruel.

Once again, I felt like my dad let me down and didn't handle my heart with loving care. I felt like he just took the pieces of my already broken heart and stomped and crushed them on the ground. This turned out to be a good and bad thing in my life. It taught me to pick up and press through and persevere through the pain, but it also didn't allow for me to learn how to grieve and go through the process of healing. It just taught me to move on and stuff my emotions. Just moving on is very detrimental to our growth.

Grief involves moving through different emotions for a purpose. The grief process helps with our emotional and spiritual development. We need the grief process for change, healing, and ongoing growth in every area of our lives. The Bible says in Psalm 34:18, *"The Lord is near the brokenhearted and saves the crushed in spirit."* When we allow ourselves to grieve, we open ourselves up for God's comfort, because He is right there, waiting to catch every tear.

The next day my mom's sisters came from Cleveland, Ohio, and had her cremated. There was no service for my mom, so I never felt like I had that closure that I needed. Once again, my experience taught me to just move on. I felt hurt and anger towards my mom's sisters, and prior to my mom's passing away, I had never met my aunts.

This was so devastating in my life that it was hard for me to see mothers and daughters together without getting a lump in my throat, just longing for that with my own mother. Then the reality would hit once again; my mom was gone. Before the fire, I somehow still had hope that my mom would get better, and she and I would have those mother-daughter talks, and my mom would help me pick out a prom and a wedding dress, and go to mother-daughter tea parties. The reality hit me that this would never happen for me.

What made matters worse was that all the photo albums were burned in the fire. We were left with only two photos of my mom that my sister had of her: one with her sitting up in her bed crocheting, and her driver's license photo. None of us had any baby pictures. To this very day I don't know what I looked like as a baby. The earliest picture that anyone has of me is 1st grade. It's so ironic that the earliest photo I have is when my innocence was taken from me in the 1st grade at 6 years of age.

This experience only added to my identity crisis, and caused me to continue to run from the pain and brokenness. I wanted so badly to be loved. I hit the streets again, trying to find a home that would fill the void and emptiness in my heart. In every home I landed in I was taught about Jesus! You see, Jesus was trying to show me that He was the only one who could fill the voids in my life. Romans 15:13: *"May the God of hope fill you with all joy and peace as you trust in Him."* "If only I would have let Him.

In one home I ran away from, their father was a deacon at the church, so they had us in church four days a week and twice on Sundays. I really enjoyed going to church and did find peace and love there, but for some reason I was still searching for the love in a person instead of accepting the true love that only Jesus can give.

I don't know if you have ever felt forsaken by God. In times of real hardship, even the most committed believers in Christ can wonder, has God forsaken me and abandoned me? You ask yourself why does God allow so much suffering? In times like this it is difficult to see God's providence and provision in your circumstances. If you have ever felt this way, you are not alone.

The good news is that God gives us encouragement in His word, especially in the story of Ruth, where we find a mother-in-law on the verge of despair and a daughter-in-law hurting and feeling lost. But Ruth took a leap of faith and committed to stick by her mother-in-law's side, knowing that she had no more sons to give in marriage.

Like Naomi, widowed and childless in a foreign land, Ruth was crying out, *"The Lord's hand has turned against me"* (Ruth 1:13b). Have you ever felt like you would have been better off if you had been born in a different family? Did you ever feel that life was unfair, that you were dealt a bad hand in life?

I was taught Psalm 27:10, *"Though your father and mother forsake you the Lord receives you."* I didn't understand it then like I do now. God knew that our earthly parents would do things that would let us down and bring disappointment to us, but He knew that He would be right there when we were ready to run into His arms.

In times of uncertainty and hardship I pray that you find comfort in knowing how God came through for Ruth and Naomi. He will also come through for you! He showed them that they weren't forsaken or abandoned. You are not forsaken; God reminds you who you are in Isaiah 62 and that He has placed watchmen on your wall that will not rest day or night until you are established. Thank you, Jesus, for the intercessors!

He is waiting to receive you today like He has received me. Thank you, Jesus, that you are our number one intercessor (Hebrews 7:25). *"Wherefore he is able also to save them to the uttermost that come unto God by him, seeing he ever lives to make intercession for them."* I now know the love of our heavenly Father, true love, and unconditional love. John 15:9 speaks, *"As the Father has loved me, so have I loved you. Abide in my love."*

Back in those days I was still searching for what was there all the time: the Father's love. This led me down a road of self-destruction, which I will speak about later in the book. Maybe you are still searching for a true love. Well, I declare today that your search is over, that Jesus is the lover of your soul. John 15:13: *"Greater love hath no man than this, that a man lay down his life for his friends."* Let this fill your heart with joy today that He calls you His friend!

Chapter 4

THE BEGINNING OF THE END

The pain was getting stronger and harder to bear since the death of my mother. The devil's voice seemed to get louder and louder, saying, "You're alone, you will never amount to anything, you can't do anything right, no one will ever love you, and you're dirty and useless." I didn't know the truth of who I was as God's daughter. I was choosing to believe the lies of the enemy. The devil comes to kill, steal, and destroy, starting with our identity. I believe that destroying our identity is actually his starting point. He plants lies in our head about our identity that are contrary to the word of God. That's why it's so important to know your God-given identity. What I know from experience is this: it not only affects what you believe about yourself, but it also influences the way you live your life. I was looking for a way to drown out that voice, and to find a way of escape to fill the pain and suffering

I rushed home from school because this was a special day. You can only imagine the anticipation I had on the inside of me because tonight was the night I was invited to go to a party. This was sure to make me feel better, and was a sure way to fill the void and emptiness. I went straight to my room to work on my outfit to wear to the party. My creative juices had been flowing all day long and I decided I was going to create a shirt that would be sure to draw the attention I was craving. I bought some iron-on letters and put them on the shirt. They boldly stated, "Cancer and my name is Tanya." There was a song out at the time, so I took the phrase from that song. Remember, I was stripped of my identity and didn't know who I was, so I identified with the devil's view of us through astrology.

My friend's mother dropped us off at the party. I was asked to dance by this teenage boy whom I thought was so cool and very good looking. I went home filled with excitement, because I felt like this is exactly what I needed in my life. He was sure to fill the void and the emptiness I felt in my heart. He had beautiful green eyes that just drew me in to him. Little did I know those very eyes that I was mesmerized by later would turn into the green-eyed monster.

I gave Vance my phone number and we met at a park close by my house the next day. We started dating, and it wasn't long before I became an abused girl friend at 16 years old. I was abused physically, mentally, and emotionally. We became sexually active, and I became pregnant at age 16. His mother worked for a hospital and said she would arrange for an abortion where she worked. I was scared and lost so I agreed to have the abortion, not knowing what I was really saying yes to. I remember coming out of the recovery room feeling so sad, guilty, and confused.

My boyfriend had come from a home with an abusive father. He was a product of divorce, and had a lot of anger. When he would get angry, he looked like the Hulk. His eyes would get this crazy look in them, and his muscles and his veins would swell up. He would often call me on the phone in the middle of the night and get angry and say he was coming to my house to beat me, and I had better come out or he would shake my whole household up. He would say I am not afraid of your dad either.

Vance's mother was a believer, and she became the mother that I looked up to. His father later remarried and became a born-again believer and a pastor. I hid the abuse from everyone and would cover up my black eyes with makeup. I constantly tasted blood in my mouth from getting backhanded in my mouth so much.

I continued to run away from home, still rebelling against my father. I ditched school a lot to be with my boyfriend. He lived in West Covina with his mother and stepfather. His father lived in Inglewood. I was drawn to his family on both sides because they were the close-knit family I longed for. I started going to Vance's dad's on the weekends and began attending the church where his dad was the founder and pastor.

I soon moved in with his father and stepmother and they agreed to help me finish school and get my life on track. I knew this was the Lord's way of wanting to fill the voids in my life with Him. I went back to school and took the GED and passed it through much prayer.

When I was younger, at the age of 13, I had received the Lord, but this time it was different. This time they asked me if I wanted to be filled with the Holy Spirit. I said yes and it was at his father's little church in Inglewood, California, that my life began to change. I was filled with the spirit of the Lord, with evidence of speaking in other tongues.

I learned what true worship really was. I was so shy, and I began asking the Lord to take the shyness away and let me be unashamed to lift my hands to worship Him and shout hallelujah to His name.

I had a hunger for the Lord, but Vance didn't. He and I were already sexually active, but I wanted to stop and get things right with the Lord. I had a heavy conviction to do so. Vance wasn't having it and I was too afraid to tell him no, for fear of getting beat. I became pregnant again at the age of 19. This time I decided to keep the baby. I was ashamed that I was living under the pastor's roof and pregnant, so I moved back home with my father. I knew this would be short lived because my dad had always told us girls if we ever got pregnant, we couldn't live in his house.

My pregnancy soon began showing and my dad looked at me one day and said you remember I said no babies in my house. I meant it. There I was, feeling rejected, lost, and abandoned with no plan. I went to the home of one of my sisters and she offered me her sofa to sleep on because she lived in a one-bedroom apartment with her family. My life sped up real fast. Suddenly, I had to make adult decisions in a teenage mind and body. My son, Solomon, was born, and I had nowhere to go because my sister said I could stay only until the baby was born. Vance's aunt took me and the baby in temporarily. He and I soon got an apartment together. When our son turned six months old his mom encouraged us to get married and wanted us to stop living in sin.

Now mind you, she had no idea about the abuse. The nightmare only got worse because now he started abusing our son. I remember when our son was only one month old, he got so angry because he woke up crying at 3am, which is normal for a baby to do, he picked him up by his onesie and threw him from the crib to the bed. When I started crying saying, he is just a baby, he started beating me.

I would forgive him time and time again because he would cry and say he didn't understand why he kept doing it. I was so afraid for my baby, but I feared for both of our lives and was afraid to leave. He soon asked me to marry him, and I said yes, but in the back of my mind I was thinking how could I love a man who beats me and my child?

Vance asked his father, the pastor, to marry us. His father was filled with the Holy Spirit and had the gift of prophecy. He pulled me aside and told me he had a word from the Lord for me. He told me that the Lord said that his son was not my husband, and I was not to marry him. He said, "Your heart is toward the Lord and his heart is far away from Him, and he is only going to lead you away from the Lord."

Oh, how I wish I could tell you that I took heed to the word of the Lord, but I didn't listen. I kept thinking to myself, I love him and how could I tell him I changed my mind about marrying him? So, I married him at the age of 20 years old. He was 19 years old. We were just two hurting kids. I regretted not listening to the Lord every day of our marriage. I had read in the word of God in 1 Samuel 15:22, *"Behold, to obey is better than sacrifice, and to hearken than the fat of rams."* Oh, how I wish I had been obedient to the Lord. The abuse only got worse, and I couldn't hide the abuse from my family any longer. My sisters would see the bruises on our son's bottom when he would take baths at their house, and I would always make excuses as to where the bruises came from. I remember coming home from work one day when Solomon was 3 years old, and he had a black eye. I asked my husband what happened and he starting crying saying I was teaching him to write his name and I got angry because he wasn't writing it correctly and I lost my temper and hit him. I remember saying that's it and I grabbed my son and said we were leaving. He started beating me, saying I wasn't going anywhere, and that he would kill me. So, there were my son and I, both with black eyes.

He always called me out of my name and told me I had no common sense. He would say, "B_____, you're not going anywhere." This abuse went on for a total of 10 years. I jumped out of the car many times when we would be at a stop light to keep from getting beaten while we were driving. I remember one time jumping out of the car at midnight. I was crying and losing blood from getting beaten. I didn't know what to do. I found this little Mormon church that was open and asked for help. What are the odds of a church being open that time of night? I really felt that it was an angel of the Lord that turned the lights on and opened the church door for me. I used the phone and called someone to pick me up.

I soon went back home because I was afraid for my son and his safety. One night he told me he was leaving and that he had had enough. He said, "Stupid B_____, pack my clothes." That was always my name when he was angry. As I started packing his clothes, he started beating me saying "B____, you were just going to let me leave?" I said, "You told me to pack your clothes." He started beating me some more saying, "B____, put my clothes back in the closet and if you ever try to leave, I will kill you."

I lived in constant fear. I remember getting in the shower and crying saying. "God, I know I don't deserve this. There must be someone out there who would love me and not abuse me." I prayed and asked God to get me out of the mess I had gotten myself into.

I am reminded of the story in the Bible of the destruction of Sodom and Gomorrah. Two angels give Lot instructions on how to flee the city (Genesis 19:15-17,26). The verse states that the angels said to Lot, *"Flee for your lives. Don't look back,"* and the Bible says that she (Lot's wife) looked back and was turned into a pillar of salt. This makes me think of the word of warning I received from my boyfriend's father. The Lord said, "this is not your husband, get out or he will take you away from God and lead you down the wrong road." The significance of this event is how God loves us so much. He tries to forewarn us to keep us from consequences that could lie ahead of us for our disobedience. We thank God today that He doesn't turn us into pillars of salt. Amen.

God's mercy and grace gives you and me another chance to flee from sin and to heed the word of the Lord that tells us, *"There is a way that seems right to a man but in the end, it leads to destruction"* (Proverbs 14:12).

If you have ever felt like me, that you have made a mess of your life because you didn't know your true identity in Christ; if you have found yourself in a place of disobedience, know that our Heavenly Father loves you with an everlasting love (Jeremiah 31:3). God says in 1 Cor. 10:13, *"No temptation has overtaken you except such is common to man; but God is faithful, who will not allow you to be tempted beyond what you are able, but with the temptation will also make the way of escape, that you may be able to bear it."*

The Bible is clear in that it promises the faithful disciples of Christ victory over sin. In other words, it is God's intention for His sons and daughters to cease completely from sin. God's will for us is to come to freedom from sin (Romans 6:12-14). He has already planned your way of escape, Hallelujah! You are coming out, I see you on the other side of this, victory is yours today!

The Beginning of the End

Chapter 5

THE TRUTH THAT FREES US

I realized the time had come and gone for my monthly cycle. I thought to myself, oh no, I am pregnant again. What am I going to do? I knew my husband, Vance, didn't want another child yet. I knew when he found out he would tell me to get an abortion. That's exactly what happened. I said we can't keep using this as a form of birth control. He yelled at me and forced me to get an abortion. Out of fear I listened to him. I was so devasted, hurt, guilty, and ashamed because this was my second abortion.

I would tell him to wait until my birth control took effect, but he never wanted to wait. He just couldn't restrain himself from having sex. Shortly after that I found out I was pregnant again and this time I said no to abortion. I just couldn't bring myself to have another abortion. It just wasn't right.

I was working for the bank in their automation department, reconciling checks. This was back in the 80's before everything was done electronically. I would lift boxes of checks in and out of these shelves. I didn't think they were too heavy. One day I started spotting blood. I was 5-1/2 months along in my pregnancy. I went to the doctor, and he told me to stop lifting the boxes and to take 3 days off work and put my feet up. I was the only one working at the time in my household. Vance had been laid off his job. I didn't want to keep missing work because my supervisor was already giving me a hard time about going to my doctor's appointments or having to miss if my son was sick. I took 2 days off and went back to work and continued lifting the boxes. I would say to myself they are not that heavy. The next day I woke up and I was cramping bad and spotting again. I went to the hospital, and they said it sounds like you are miscarrying, they told me there was nothing they could do, for me to go home and rest and let it take its course. I went home and the cramping got worse. I jumped up thinking I had to urinate, and I sat on the toilet and the baby came out in the toilet. I looked down and I screamed when I saw the underdeveloped fetus. The head was big, and the eyes were big it looked like the pictures I had seen of the process of a baby's development. I told Solomon to get the cordless phone for me so I could call 911. When the ambulance arrived, they cut the umbilical cord and they rushed me to the hospital. They took me into surgery to perform a DNC to remove tissue in the uterus and small pieces of placenta that remained after childbirth.

Having a miscarriage is identical to the loss of a child and is very traumatic. I had to allow myself to grieve by expressing my emotions, but I really just wanted to crawl into a hole and never come out. I went home that afternoon in so much pain. I was also feeling heartbroken and so guilty for not listening to the doctor's orders. I also started developing resentment and bitterness for my children's father, because I also felt like all the stress and physical, mental, and emotional abuse contributed to the miscarriage.

I soon returned to work and tried to pick up the pieces of my broken heart. If you are experiencing the grief of a miscarriage, or you are the father of a child that was miscarried, give yourself time. Talk to understanding friends and family, but you can't rush the grief process. *God is near the broken hearted and the crushed in spirit* (Psalm 34:18). Allow God to take you through the process of healing. I am so thankful God got me through the process.

A month and a half later I found out I was pregnant again. I was still working for the bank but this time I would be smarter and not do any lifting because I didn't want to miscarry again. I asked to be moved to another department and my request was granted.

You see, I learned my lesson the hard way but thank God I learned and didn't repeat it again. You can't learn anything from a mistake until you admit that you made it. So, take a deep breath and admit it to yourself and then take ownership of it like I did. I went through so much emotional and mental anguish during that time over the abortions and the miscarriage. I felt like God was mad at me for killing my babies. I wasn't given the truth at the abortion clinics, they would always tell me it's just tissue, it's not a baby yet, it's just a fetus. They put in your mind you are not killing a baby if you have an abortion before 12 weeks of pregnancy. I now know the truth that life begins at fertilization with the embryo's conception.

The devil uses people to blind you to the truth as we see in 2 Corinthians 4:4. *"In their case the god of this world has blinded the minds of unbelievers, to keep them from seeing the light of the gospel of the glory of Christ, who is the image of God."* In Exodus 20:13, the Bible says, *"You shall not murder."* I knew that the truth was that the devil had lied to me and deceived me. I had murdered my babies.

For years I carried around guilt and shame and kept it a secret. To be honest, to this day I have a hard time telling people how many abortions I've had, but I tell the devil to shut up, because I know I am forgiven. The devil used it to torment me. What you keep in the dark the devil has access to use. He operates in darkness, and he doesn't want you to bring it out into the light because he will lose his power over you. Acts 26:18 says, *"To open their eyes, so that they may turn from darkness to light and from the power of Satan to*

God, that they may receive forgiveness of sins and a place among those who are sanctified by faith in me."

I ran into the arms of Jesus, asking Him for forgiveness. I knew I was forgiven because He says in 1 John 1:9, *"If we confess our sins, he is faithful and just and will forgive us our sins and purify us from all unrighteousness."* He will cast all our sins into the depths of the sea. Psalm 103:12 expresses it like this: *"As far as the east is from the west, so far has He removed our transgressions from us."* A sea of forgetfulness represents a place where our sins are sent very far away from us, so that they can no longer affect us. Although our sins still grieve God and cause ruin in our lives and in the lives of others, the idea that our sins are lost in a sea of forgetfulness is a comfort.

Romans 8:1 admonishes us, *"There is therefore now no condemnation to them which are in Christ Jesus."* That truth frees us to live life in a way that pleases God. Spiritual growth requires that we recognize the total forgiveness that exists in Jesus Christ and that we rest in that forgiveness.

If you have been plagued by the guilt and shame of abortion, whether you had an abortion, or if you were the father of a child that was aborted, I want you to know that there is forgiveness in Christ Jesus! The good news is that one day you will see your child/children again in heaven. 2 Corinthians 5:8 says, *"We are confident, I say, and willing*

35

rather to be absent from the body, and to be present with the Lord." I like how Micah 7:19 puts it: *"He will again have compassion on us and will subdue our iniquities."* Micah was a true prophet of God. He was willing to pay any personal price to perform his ministry, even to being stripped naked for the sake of the message.

We must be willing to allow God to use our testimonies for His glory, knowing the truth and being unashamed of our past (Revelation 12:11). Micah's words should help us understand and marvel at our relationship with the Lord Jesus Christ and the compassion that He has toward us.

Psalm 103:8-11: *"The Lord is merciful and gracious, slow to anger and abounding in mercy. He will not always strive with us, nor will he keep his anger forever. He has not dealt with us according to our sins, nor punished us according to our iniquities. For as the heavens are high above the earth, so great is His mercy toward those who fear him."* We are free because of His blood that He shed for us. Free from moral and religious sins, just as the people in Micah's day experienced freedom from greed and idolatry as they followed God.

The abortion industry is about greed and idolatry at the expense of innocent babies. Micah's generation was run by faithless rulers interested only in money or personal gain

(Micah 3:9-12). Just as our nation is being run the same way, but like Micah did, we must keep praying for our nation. The Lord's salvation is our nation's only hope.

God has chosen you; you have overcome all that you have been through for such a time as this. You are useful to the Kingdom of God. You are not dirty but clean, washed by the blood of the Lamb (1 Corinthians 6:10-11). You are fit for the Master's use; He has prepared you for every good work (2 Timothy 3:16-17). Amen.

Chapter 6

GOD MADE A WAY OF ESCAPE

I rushed out of the house for work. I had nothing in the refrigerator to prepare for lunch, so I took the last $5.00 to get myself something to eat. I received a call at work, and they said your husband is on the phone. I picked up the phone and said hello, and all I could hear was screaming and cussing. He said, "B_____, you took the last $5.00. That was for my beer. I am going to f___ you up when I pick you up from work." I was trying so hard to fight back the tears at work. I asked him, "Did you forget I am pregnant, and I must eat?" He said, "B_____, I don't care. No one told you to have that baby anyway."

I was so nervous and upset all day long thinking about the beating I was going to get when he picked me up. I could hardly hold it together and was fighting back the tears all day. It was time to clock out for the day. I walked out of my job to my husband waiting in the car for me. We didn't make it out of the parking lot good before he backhanded me in the face and said, "B_____, don't you ever take my money that is for my beer." I was crying and shaking and when he raised his hand I jumped. He said, "B_____, what are you jumping for? I wasn't going to hit you again but since you jumped," and before I knew it, he had back handed me again and dared me to jump again. You could only imagine the turmoil my son was going through on the inside of me.

The abuse continued. I am surprised none of the neighbors ever called the police. I was now 8-1/2 months pregnant. I began noticing that when I would roll over in the middle of the night my husband would not be in bed or at home for that matter. I began sensing that something was going on, but I didn't know what. He had friends in the apartment building we lived in and would often hang out with them and drink and smoke marijuana. I remember one night waking up at 3am and he wasn't home, so I walked outside to see if he was out there. I saw him walking home with no shirt or shoes on. I said, "Where have you been?" and he said he got drunk and fell asleep at his friend's house. I felt like something just wasn't adding up. I tried to lay down and get a few hours of sleep because I knew my alarm clock would be going off soon and it would be time to get ready for work.

It was my 24th birthday and through all the sadness and turmoil in my life, I mustarded up enough from within me to be excited about my birthday. My husband dropped me off for work that day like any normal day, I thought. I was not prepared for what was about to happen next. When I clocked out for work, he was waiting for me. I tried to perkup and asked him what we were going to do for my birthday. He said, "You are pregnant. We can't do anything fun." I said, "We can go for pizza, and you can get yourself a pitcher of beer while our son plays video games in the arcade." He said, "No, I don't feel like doing that," so I made a couple of other suggestions and he shut them down. I started tearing up and feeling sad, sensing something is just not right. I told him to just stop at Taco Bell and get Solomon and me something to eat. He pulled into the liquor store parking lot and bought himself a case of beer before taking us to pick up our food.

As we pulled into the parking lot of our apartment complex, I remember seeing an acquaintance of mine and her daughter in the parking lot. Her daughter was riding her big wheel and she was sitting in a lounge chair. We got out of the car and went into the house. He took his case of beer and immediately went outside. I didn't think anything of it at first. My son sat down to eat. He soon said he was full and asked if he could go outside with his dad. I told him to go ahead, relieved that I could let some of the tears drop that I had been holding in. He quickly came back inside, and I asked him why he came back in the house, and he said his dad said he needed to stay inside. I immediately remembered who was outside when we drove into the apartments. I said, "Son, does it have anything to do with

Rhonda?" He began to shake and cry and say, "Mom, I can't tell you. Daddy said he would spank me all the days of my life if I tell you."

Now I really had to know what was going on. My adrenaline was really going. I am not proud of what I did next. I bribed my son with buying him a new toy if he told me what was going on. I promised him I wouldn't tell his dad. I took my son across the street to the liquor store and bought him a toy. When we came back home, he sat down and began to talk to me like an adult, not a 4-1/2-year-old little boy. Solomon had always been wise beyond his years. He said, "Mom, one day you were at work and Rhonda and her daughter followed me and my dad to granny's house. When we arrived there, my dad told me and her daughter to go and sit downstairs in the den to watch cartoons. He told me him and Rhonda were going upstairs to talk. Mom, they weren't going upstairs to talk."

I just remember seeing red. I can't explain it but that's all I saw. Hurt, anger, and rage began to rise on the inside of me. I had promised my son if he told me I wouldn't tell his dad but all that went out the window. Now mind you I am 8-1/2 months pregnant with our second son. I sat my son down and opened his new toy and told him to sit down and play with it and that mommy would be right back. I had a cutlery set in the kitchen and I grabbed the biggest knife that was in it. I put the knife under my shirt inside my pants and stormed outside.

This is where I want to pause my story for a moment and talk to you about abuse, anger, rage, bitterness, and resentment. If you are in a physically abusive marriage or relationship, whether you are a male or female, you must get help. You might have to separate for a season so that the abuser can get help. You must get help yourself from a professional trained to get victims out safely who are in domestic violence. Oftentimes fear and threats are instilled in victims of abuse. That is why it is not always easy to get out, but with God nothing shall be impossible (Matthew 19:26).

Everyone deserves a relationship free from domestic violence. God would not have us to be beaten and abused. 1 Corinthians 6:19 says; *"Do you not know that your body is a temple of the Holy Spirit who is in you, whom you have received from God? You are not your own."* There is no verse in the Bible that condones spousal abuse. God hates violence.

In Genesis 6:13 we read, *"And God said unto Noah, the end of all flesh is come before me; for the earth is filled with violence through them; and behold, I will destroy them with the earth."* God hates abuse so much that because of violence He destroyed all but eight people that were once on the earth. The earth was full of people who used fear and force through violence so God from heaven destroyed them.

There was a pattern of behavior of fear and physical force. In Psalm 11:5 we read, *"The Lord trieth the righteous: but the wicked and him that loveth violence his soul hateth."* When you stay in a relationship like this you become resentful and angry and if left unchecked, that bitter root grows up inside of you. That spirit of anger and rage can turn into a spirit of murder. I knew I had resentment, bitterness, anger, and rage on the inside of me for my husband, because of all the abuse. God wanted to deliver me and heal me. He sent many people in my path to help me out, but I rejected it. Many times, when you allow this bitter root to grow in you, you can become like the very person you resented and the very thing that hurt you. So much so that you begin to now turn it on someone else.

Let's get back to the story. I went outside and I started walking toward the parking lot where I remember Rhonda was sitting outside with her daughter. As I was walking by the children's playground Rhonda was walking toward me. She looked very shocked to see me. I vaguely remember children in the playground because I was in such a rage. I grabbed her and said, "B_____, you have been sleeping with my husband." She started denying it and I told her my 4-year- old son could never make a story up like that. I grabbed the knife out of my pants and just as I did my husband walked up and saw what was going on. He grabbed me around the neck and took the knife out of my hands. Now you can see what I am talking about how quickly the spirit of murder came in. Thank you, Jesus, that he sent my husband at the right time to stop me from committing murder. That would have changed me and my children's lives forever.

You might be saying to yourself this will never be me but let me tell you it can happen so fast and before you know it, this can be you. No one could have ever told me I would ever attempt something like that. That was a real wake up call for me. Don't ignore the warning signs. They are always there. I hope in this moment this is a wakeup call for you. God made a way of escape for me that day. He wants to make a way of escape for you.

It's not by accident that you are reading this book, if not for you, maybe for a friend or a loved one. We read in 1 Corinthians 10:13, "*There hath no temptation taken you, but such as is common to man: but God is faithful, who will not suffer you to be tempted above that ye are able; but will with the temptation also make a way to escape, that ye may be able to bear it.*"

My husband started dragging me in the house telling Rhonda, "I am so sorry for all of this. I don't know why she would believe a 4-year-old." I was yelling and screaming. I had never ever talked back to him before. All of that pent up anger and bitterness was now being released in the wrong way.

The Bible tells us in Ephesians 4:26, *"Be ye angry, and sin not."* Hebrews 12:15 says, <u>"Looking diligently lest any man fail in the grace of God; lest any root of bitterness springing up trouble you, and thereby many be defiled."</u> Boy was there trouble, and many were defiled in that moment. This was not at all the way I thought I would spend my 24th birthday. Rhonda followed us as he dragged me into the house. He started beating me, kicking me and at the same time telling Rhonda, I am so sorry, I don't know why she believes a 4-year-old child. I was screaming, "B____, get out of my house." I was so afraid he was going to make me have another miscarriage. He kept hitting me and stomping me. I said, "You are going to make me lose the baby, and he said, "I don't care, B____. I didn't want the bastard anyway."

I thought to myself, I have got to get out of here. This had triggered his rage now. I knew I had to think fast to save my baby's life. I lied and told him that I had called his mom and she was on her way. He snapped out of the rage for a minute, and I got up, grabbed my son by the hand, and started walking as fast as I could down the walkway. He called Solomon and said, "Get back here now." My son pulled away from me and ran back to his dad. I believe he

46

ran back out of fear. I was so afraid for my son because I knew his dad would make good on his promise that if he told me what was going on he would beat him.

I ran to the gas station that was next door to our apartment complex. I was hysterical, and I said, "Please help me." I had blood on my face because he had busted my lip, and my face was swollen from him back handing me. The gas station attendant said, "Are you ok? What happened?" I told him my husband had done this to me. I asked him if he would please just call the police for me. When the police arrived I told them my husband had beat me and they said do you want to press charges? I told them, "No. Can you just please take me to my mother-in-law's house?" They said, "Ma'am, are you sure?" I said, "Yes, can you please hurry I have to get back to my son."

When I arrived at her house, she answered the door and I proceeded to tell her what happened. I said, "We have to hurry, he is going to hurt Solomon for telling me." When we were pulling into the parking lot of the apartment complex there was my son sitting, looking out the window as if waiting for me to come back for him. I saw a big red mark on his face and immediately knew he had slapped him in the face for telling me. I felt so bad for not handling it differently.

We went to the door, and it was locked, I didn't have my keys, so his mother and I knocked on the door. He answered, and his mother started saying, "What is wrong with you? Why would you do this to your family?" As she was speaking, Solomon ran to the door and tried to run to his grandmother. My husband pushed his mother and started cussing, telling our son to go back into the house. His mother started tussling with him, and I grabbed Solomon and his mom told him she was going to call the police, but to our surprise one of the neighbors finally called the police. The police arrived and convinced Vance to let Solomon go with me.

My son and I spent the night at his mom's house. That night I couldn't eat or sleep. My world had just been turned upside down. I took my wedding ring off and then put it on, contemplating if I was going to forgive him and stay in the marriage.

His mother's phone lines happened to be down so her phone wasn't working. I desperately longed to talk to a friend, to find some relief and comfort. Everyone in the house was asleep but me. I quietly creeped down the stairs at 1 am in the morning. My husband's mom lived up a hill and the store was far from her house. I was so distraught I didn't care at that moment; my emotions were all over the place. I wasn't even thinking about the dangers of walking the streets that time of night, I just wanted to get to a pay phone. I called who I thought was my best friend in the apartments, and to my surprise, she had betrayed me too. She told me that the whole complex just about knew what was going on but me. I said, "Why didn't you tell me?" She said, "I didn't want to tell you because you were pregnant, and I didn't want to upset you."

My so-called friend said that my husband and Rhonda had been meeting up at her house in the evenings, but her husband told her not to tell me. I felt like I had a double whammy. First, my husband betrays me, and then someone I considered a best friend betrays me.

I hung up the phone, feeling worse than when I put myself and my baby in danger, walking the streets that time of night. Thank God, for I know His angels were watching over me; I made it back to his mom's home safely.

The next day I asked his mother to take me to my house to get some clothes because she had told me to stay at her house for a couple of days and let things cool off. His mother went up to the door with me. Vance answered, and he said, "Tanya, can we talk?" His mother said, "No, Tanya. Just get your clothes; it's only going to upset you." I didn't listen. I insisted that I would be ok. I just wanted to hear him out.

When I went in to talk to him, he confessed that it was true what our son had told me. He was having an affair with Rhonda. I was ready to forgive him and thought we would get past the betrayal. What he told me next devastated me. He said that he was in love with Rhonda and was going to move in with her, and that he would still be there when it was time for our son to be born. I begged him not to do this to our family, but he insisted that he loved her.

When I went back to his mom's car, I was hysterical, and she basically said I told you so. His mother told me not to ask him to do anything for me, that she would be there for me if I needed to run errands. For the life of me I don't know why I didn't listen. I had received shut off notices for the utilities and phone bill. I had just received my paycheck and Vance came by and asked me if I needed anything and I said, "Yes. If I give you the money can you go and pay the utilities and the phone bill before they get shut off?" He agreed, but when he arrived back at Rhonda's house, my sisters were so angry about what he was doing to me, they went to give Vance and Rhonda a piece of their minds. The police were called and one of my sisters went to jail for disturbing the peace.

A couple of days went by, and I realized my utilities and phone were shut off. I asked Vance, "Didn't you pay the bills? Everything is shut off." He said, "Rhonda was so upset about your sisters coming over and was afraid for her life, so I took her to a hotel on the beach with the money you gave me for the bills." Talk about a slap in the face, but that's what happens when you receive Godly counsel and don't listen.

I called his mom only to hear I told you so. I guess I deserved that. I had just enough money to get the utilities turned back on but not enough for the phone bill, so I left it off. I cried for days, but one day I woke up and I started thinking that maybe him cheating on me and leaving me was a blessing in disguise. I started thinking maybe God knew I would never leave him and would stay in this abusive marriage forever, so God allowed all of this to happen to rescue me, to give me a way of escape. God rescued me from not only committing murder but from being an abused and battered wife.

Let him rescue you, a friend, or loved one today. I am not proud of this story, but I want someone to allow God to spare them from doing something that they will regret. Remember, no one loves you like God, for He is love (1 John 4:16) and you are the beloved of God!

Abuse is not love, and there is nothing you can do or say to deserve it. God gives us a picture of what love is in 1 Corinthians 13:4-7, "*Love is patient, love is kind. It does not envy, it does not boast, it is not proud. It does not dishonor others, it is not self-seeking, it is not easily angered, it keeps no record of wrongs.*"

God Made a Way of Escape

Chapter 7

TRAUMA TO REBOUND TO TRIUMPH

All the trauma of these events began to take a toll on the pregnancy. I started losing weight from all the stress and the doctor told me that I should be gaining and not losing weight. He asked me what was going on? I told him I had no appetite, and that I was going through a divorce with my husband. I had planned to work through my whole pregnancy, but the doctor said I want you to take your maternity leave now, and focus on bringing in a healthy baby. I listened to the doctor's advice. I started slowly picking up the pieces of my broken heart.

One of my neighbors invited me to church, so I started looking to God to get me through it. I started having Braxton Hicks contractions and I had a couple of false alarms, thinking I was in labor, but when my husband took me to the hospital, they said I was not in labor yet.

One night I couldn't sleep. I was tossing and turning and was getting some sharp pains. I tried to go back to sleep but I started getting contractions every five minutes. Somehow, I knew this is the real thing and I knew that I was in labor. I woke Solomon up because remember, I no longer had a telephone. I asked him to go with me to his dad's house because I was in so much pain. I knew I couldn't climb the stairs. My poor son was so sleepy, but he went up the stairs and knocked on the door. When his dad answered the door Solomon told him, "Mom is going to have the baby and she needs you to take her to the hospital." His dad told him that he would get dressed and be right there.

A long period of time went by, and I was wondering what was taking him so long to come. The next thing I knew his mom was at the door. I wanted to know why she had come. She said, "I was asked to take you to the hospital and to call your husband if it is the real thing, and he will come."

My heart sunk to the floor; I was so hurt. We arrived at the hospital and indeed I was in labor, so I told her to go call my husband and let him know. Hours went by and he still had not come to the hospital. I asked his mom over and over where he was. She said not to worry about him because she was there for me. I told her that I wanted him there when the baby was born, and she said, "Tanya, I didn't want to tell you, but he is not coming." I started crying and asked why. She told me that Rhonda wouldn't let him come. I said, "What, and he is listening to her?"

I thought, what kind of woman would stop a man from seeing his child born. They had the baby on the monitor, and they told me he was sunny side up instead of face down. They tried everything to get him to turn over, but he just wasn't budging. I thought to myself, my son is trying to look up to figure out what in the world is going on out there with my mom and dad; what kind of world am I coming into?

It was hard. They had to use forceps to help pull him out because he was stuck, which made for a more painful delivery. But I got through it with the Lord's strength, and Daniel was born. It was a bittersweet moment. I was so happy to see my son but sad about his dad not being there. I had cried so much and so hard the last month and a half of my pregnancy. I would cry until no sound would come out — just a deep breath, sigh, and a moan would be all I had left.

When it came time for my son and me to leave the hospital, they said my son may have to stay because he is not breathing right, and something may be wrong with his lungs. They wanted to run some tests to make sure. The nurse came in and said, "Listen to his breathing." I told her, "Nothing is wrong with his lungs. He is just crying my cry that he picked up in the womb the last month and a half, that's it. All I did was cry myself to sleep." The doctors ran tests and couldn't find anything wrong with his heart or lungs, so they released him to go home with me. It took about 3 months for him to stop sighing and moaning in his sleep.

Things were hard at home because Rhonda didn't want my husband to come over and see the baby. She said he had to bring the baby to her house. I didn't want my newborn baby going over to her house. Honestly, I think the main reason was out of resentment toward her. My husband didn't spend that much time with the baby at first. I eventually gave in and allowed him to take the baby to her house with him.

The abuse continued even though he no longer lived in our home. It was time for me to return to work, so I bought myself some new clothes and went and got my hair styled. I started feeling good about myself again.

Life was hard. I would often walk to the grocery store with the kids and push the grocery cart back from the store. Because he had torn down my self-esteem, I never got a driver's license while I was with him, mainly because every time he took me out to practice driving, I would get backhanded if I made the smallest mistake, so I gave up. But God made a way. He blessed me with co-workers who would pick me and my children up, drop them off at daycare and the babysitter, and give me a ride to work.

I would have to get my 4-1/2-year-old up at 5am to get himself dressed and have him feed his baby brother while I got dressed for work. I remember he would be half asleep feeding his brother, but he was a good big brother.

I eventually returned to church and the Lord began tugging at my heart to tell my husband and Rhonda that I forgave them for all the hurt and pain they caused me. I chose to walk in obedience, and I told them I forgave them. To my surprise they both apologized for what they had done to hurt me. I felt so free, but eventually the heart of forgiveness all faded away when I stopped going to church before the Lord could complete the healing I so needed. I was trying to get over this soap opera of a life, but that could only be possible if I continued following the Lord.

One day I saw a big banner over Rhonda's front door that said it's a boy. I was devastated. I was like oh no; they are having a baby. Jealousy, hurt, pain, and resentment came rushing into my heart. I felt even more embarrassed now because our sons would be a year apart.

My friend knew I was heartbroken over the news, so she said you need to get out of the house and do something fun to get your mind off them. She invited me to go out to make me feel better. I remember going skating one night and ran into a guy that I knew from high school. We exchanged phone numbers and we began dating. Within 3 months I let him move in with me and the kids. I allowed the devil to set me up again. I was on the rebound; what a mess. I had my husband living with his mistress upstairs and now me downstairs living with my boyfriend. Talk about a soap opera! What talk must have been going on in our apartment complex.

One day my husband and I got into a big argument outside over our son. If I were to be honest, it was my fault because I was a woman scorned. I realized in that moment I was still so angry with him and wanted him to hurt like I hurt. All he had done was pick up our son and proceeded to take him to Rhonda's house, and I tried to grab our son from him, and there was this tug of war. My boyfriend came outside, and there was a big fight, and they both went to jail that day. My boyfriend started telling me it was time for us to move, and I agreed that would be best. I found another apartment and we moved out a month later.

It felt so good to get away from all that turmoil that I was living in every day. My life still was not on the right track because I was still living in sin with my boyfriend. Things were bad at home; my boyfriend was always cheating on me with other women, and life was one big party for him. He was a good provider, but he had his own demons and insecurities. He was very possessive and controlling. These were warning signs that should never have been ignored by either of us. Possessiveness is not love; it is simply projected fear and insecurity. I am no professional or expert, but from my experience, this leads to serious problems like jealousy, abuse, paranoia, and stalking, just to name a few. I experienced them all from him.

Possessiveness in relationships stems from insecurities, of which the root cause is often the fear of abandonment, helplessness, and rejection. You talk about a toxic relationship where we both had trust issues, a spirit of abandonment, and rejection on us. He was abandoned by his father at the age of 2 years old and abandoned by his mother during his last year of high school.

He wasn't physically abusive in the beginning. I was the aggressive one because of the abuse I came out of, but he was very verbally abusive and very degrading. He would come home after having sex with another woman and then force himself on me. I would try to fight him off and he would force me to have sex with him. He would literally rape me with force. He would often throw his beer in my face when he couldn't control me. If he didn't like something I was wearing he would rip my shirt off me and get scissors and cut my shorts up. If he felt I was giving too much attention to a conversation with someone of the opposite sex he would explode.

He went from being emotionally, mentally, and sexually abusive to becoming physically abusive. The children would witness all of the arguing and fighting. I knew how bad this was because of what they had already gone through with their dad. I went through this for 10 years before I got out. You would have thought I had had enough the first 10 years with my husband Vance, but when you don't get healed, this is what happens. You end up on the rebound. You are trying to get over one hurt, thinking putting someone in their place will fix everything. What really happens is you get the same type of person with a different name.

This reminds me of the children of Israel. They made an 11-day journey turn into 40 years around the mountain. Instead of 40 years mine was a 20-year journey around the mountain and out of bondage.

I started going back to church again, knowing that Jesus was my only way out. I would get really convicted while at church. Somehow when I would go, the subject of adultery and living in sin with someone you are not married to would always come up. We all know how the Lord has a way of getting His message to us at the right time.

I would come home and ask him to leave, only to let him beg me to come back within a couple of days. I decided that I couldn't fight this alone, so I went up for prayer at the church and asked them to pray that I would be strong enough not to keep taking him back. One day when I was on the phone with my friend, Opal, he had been drinking and smoking marijuana. He knew my friend was always telling me I needed to get out of this toxic relationship. She would tell me that I deserved better. He felt threatened that one day

I would take her advice. He got mad and snatched the telephone out of my hand and threw it in the bathroom sink, grabbed me by my shirt, and started yelling at me. He threw me down on the couch and started choking me. This was the first time he went from grabbing and pushing to something serious. My son was screaming, and he let me go. I reached for the phone to call the police, but he overpowered me and took it and threw it, and broke it this time.

Solomon ran to the neighbors and called the police. When they arrived, I asked them to remove him from my house. Thank the Lord, I had not put him on the lease agreement with me. They made him take all his belongings and leave. I walked into the bathroom, and before I could turn the light on, the Lord said, "Look at what he is doing to you." I looked in the mirror and all I saw a was a skeleton.

I screamed because I didn't see my skin, just a skeleton, and the Lord said, "This is what he is doing to you, he is literally killing you inside." I knew this was it. I could never take him back. I surrendered to the Lord fully, and the effectual fervent prayers of the righteous did avail much, just like the Word says in James 5:16.

I never took him back. Praise the Lord! I was so thankful for the intercessors who prayed me out. I made my triumphant exit for good that time! When God makes a way of escape for you, you can and will be delivered! Galatians

5:1 says, *"Stand fast therefore in the liberty by which Christ has made us free, and do not be entangled again with a yoke of bondage."* I had allowed myself to get entangled again, but God was so merciful and so faithful to bring me out again.

If you have found yourself entangled in the yoke of bondage, God wants to untangle you today. You cannot do this alone. Ask God to send you some strong prayer warriors who will stay on the wall and pray for you, and not rest until your *"righteousness goes forth as brightness, and salvation thereof as a lamp that burneth"* (Isaiah 62:1).

So, let's recap the last two chapters. I am confident through *Christ you will learn from my mistakes. Ephesians 3:20 says, "Now unto him that is able to do exceedingly abundantly above all that we ask or think, according to the power that worketh in us."* The power of God is at work in you right now, my brother, my sister. I was in disobedience to the Lord when He told me that Vance was not my husband and I married him anyway. God made a way of escape for me to get out of the abusive marriage.

I ran back into the arms of Jesus. Remember, Jesus is married to the backslider (Jeremiah 3:14). When God began the healing in me, it got painful, and I ran back to the world. I allowed the devil to ensnare me again.

I rebounded into another relationship, and to make matters worse, I lived in sin with him. It is never good to be on the rebound. Usually, you rebound into a new relationship to avoid processing or resolving the emotions surrounding the breakup. It's like a death. You must go through the grieving process. You cannot skip over this process. You must process the disappointment, betrayal, sadness, pain, and hurt. Don't give in to the need to distract yourself from the hurt. Face it head-on.

James 4:7 says, *"Be subject therefore unto God. Resist the devil and he will flee from you."* Instead of resisting, I started feeling sorry for myself and wanted someone to make me feel good about myself again, to feel valued and loved instead of having the feelings I had of rejection, abandonment, and the belief that I wasn't good enough and that I didn't measure up.

God makes a way for us to come out of the trap and the lie that ensnare us. 2 Timothy 2:25-26 says, *"God may perhaps grant them repentance leading to the knowledge of the truth, and they may come to their senses and escape from the snare of the devil, after being captured by him to do his will."*

It's the lies we believe from the devil that ensnare us. I speak into your spirit man right now; I cancel every lie the devil has told you. You're not rejected but loved by the almighty God. You're enough and you are the apple of God's eye.

Deuteronomy 32:10: "He found him in a desert land, he found him in a barren and howling wilderness, he instructed him, he kept him as the apple of his eye." Moses is describing God's care for Israel. The apple of one's eye refers to the pupil, which is very sensitive. When something is coming toward our face, our natural reflexes are to close our eyes and turn our body, and our hands automatically go up in front of our face to protect ourselves. Our body naturally protects that sensitive spot to prevent injury. Now, if God says we are the apple of His eye, He holds us in a very sensitive and protected area. It's amazing to know that we are that precious to our heavenly *Father.*

There is a prayer in Psalm 17:8: "Keep me as the apple of your eye; hide me in the shadow of your wings from the wicked who are out to destroy me, from my mortal enemies who surround me." What was King David saying? God, protect us, guard us as you would the pupil of your own eye. Your process has already begun; your journey from trauma, to rebound to triumph! Whether you are at the beginning, middle, or the end of your journey to triumph, know this, the power is already in you! No need to fear; your God will fight for you, you need only to be still! (Exodus 14:14).

Chapter 8

HEALING, WHOLENESS, AND PURPOSE

It was time to face my fears and put my trust and confidence in the Lord. Proverbs 3:5-6 says, *"Trust in the Lord with all your heart and lean not on your own understanding."*

I had a fear of driving because my self-esteem was so low that I didn't think I could pass the test. I was praying and asking God to give me courage, faith, and trust that I could do it through Him. Well, at 34 years old, I finally got my license. Hallelujah!

Amid all that was going on, I was having a hard time keeping babysitters, so I resigned from my job at the bank to take care of my children. I had no child support, so I ended up on welfare. I started working part time jobs here and there, but always felt that there was something more I should be doing.

When I left my boyfriend, my sons were 10 and 15 years old. I was working for Albertsons in their customer service department, and then transferred to the bakery department. This was not a good decision because that would mean I would have to be at work at 4:30 am to have the donuts out by 6:00 am when the store opened. My children had now become latch-key kids. I would set the alarm for Solomon to get Daniel up for school, feed him, and get him dressed. Oftentimes, Solomon would oversleep, and sometimes it was just too much responsibility for him to handle, which was understandable. He was only 15 years old. I worked most weekends and missed mostly all their football games. Eventually I left that job, and I was back on welfare.

I didn't like being on welfare. I didn't want to be another statistic of single mothers on welfare. I started praying, asking the Lord what my purpose on this earth was, telling Him that I was tired of going from job to job.

I was a volunteer in the children's Sunday School Department at our church, and I really enjoyed working with the children. I also volunteered in my sons' classrooms at their schools, and helped with study groups and organizing class parties. The staff at their schools would always tell me to go apply at the school district for a teacher's assistant position. I always blew it off, thinking I am just here for my kids. I didn't realize God was speaking through them, that all along God was answering my prayers about my purpose.

The government started a welfare to work program and if you were on welfare for a year or longer you had to enroll in the program, or they would cut off your checks. The program was to teach you how to create a resume, fill out a job application, and how to dress and conduct yourself on an interview. I was so mad that they were making me enroll in this program. I thought to myself, I already know how to do all these things. I never thought myself as a prideful person, but God revealed that to me as I started the program. I went in with the wrong attitude. When the instructors would ask why I was there, I would say because it is mandatory. I remember just slouching down in the chair and one day I heard the Lord say, "Sit up and pay attention. You don't know it all." I started coming with a better attitude and even started enjoying the training I was receiving. I was at the end of the training and now it was time to sit with a counselor to talk to them about my skills and passion.

At my meeting with the counselor, they asked me what I enjoyed doing, and before I knew it, I told them I enjoyed working with children. They said they would like to put me in an internship program at an adult school that has a childcare program on campus. They gave me an address and the name of the contact person. When I arrived, they began to show me around, but the director said, "Before I can let you start interning here you must take my child development class, which is right next door." I agreed, and in that moment I said, "God, you are funny. You had a plan all along to push me into my purpose and I was resisting the process."

The funny thing is that I didn't know that this child development class would lead me to college, which I never had any aspiration of achieving. After I finished her class, she said, "I am going to transfer these units over to the college and you can finish taking the other child development courses there." Just like that, I was in college. The Bible says in Proverbs 16:9, "*The heart of a man plans his way, but the Lord establishes his steps.*"

I soon received enough Early Childhood Development units to qualify to start teaching at a childcare facility. I was so excited because, you see, I never would have thought in my wildest dreams I would be called a teacher, and they called me "Teacher Tanya." I never thought I would be leading anything or anybody. My self-esteem had been so low, but now it was being built up through God.

I want to rest here for a minute because so many of you are dealing with low self-esteem. Low self-esteem blinds you to the truth. It doesn't allow you to have confidence about who you are and what you can do. It makes you feel incompetent, unloved, or inadequate. People who struggle with low self-esteem are constantly afraid about making mistakes or letting other people down. You must change the perception of your worth, stop placing a higher value on what you think about yourself, or what people think about you, over what God thinks about you.

Take a moment and really think about what you are doing when you place your own opinion and other people's opinions about you higher than God's opinion of you. Our value is rooted in Christ. The impossible becomes possible with Christ. Give up thinking it's impossible for me to achieve financial freedom, be free from health issues, to find the right relationship, to step into my destiny or calling, etc. The moment you give up and lose hope is the moment you give your power away.

Matthew 19:26 says, "*With man this is impossible, but with God all things are possible.*" Impossible is what low self-esteem speaks to you in your mind, and if you let that voice speak louder than God, it will take away your faith that is needed for God to make the impossible possible in your life. All of us have experienced and carry scars that no one can see. These scars come from people who were in our lives and still may be a part of our life now. It's only human nature for us to formulate our self-worth based on things that have happened in our past or are happening now in the present. We also form our self-worth based on the people in our lives who played a key role in that hurt. Don't rob yourself of a life filled with joy and beauty that God wants you to experience!

The way we think about ourselves will determine the way we deal with everything that happens in our life. Remember in the last chapter I told you I began to feel sorry for myself. If you constantly have that victim mentality you will think that none of God's promises for your life will ever come to pass. You will start saying things like, "Nothing good ever comes my way." If you constantly look for all the negative things in your life or believe that you are not worthy of love, mercy, grace, and the blessings of God, you will continue to limit yourself and allow the devil to rob you of the beautiful life God intends for you. John 10:10 says, *"The thief cometh only to steal kill and destroy; I have come that they may have life, and have it to the full."*

I started seeing what God had put in me all along. I believe you are getting a clear picture now of what God sees in you too! Jeremiah 1:5: *"I knew you before I formed you in your mother's womb, before you were born, I set you apart; I appointed you as a prophet to the nations."*

Let the healing begin! It's time for you to find that inner strength to move beyond the pain in order to find inner peace and freedom. Isaiah 26:3: *"You will keep in perfect peace those whose minds are steadfast, because they trust you."*

Moving into purpose requires a different response to pain that has been inflicted on you. It's about what you do with the pain to transform your life and the lives of others. You can't control the past or what happened to you, but you can control how you respond and your view of the future.

You can act and move past what happened. God is saying to you just like He asked the man at the pool of Bethesda, in John 5:6, *"Do you want to be made whole?"*

Maybe you are saying to yourself, "You don't know what I have been through or the pain I am in right now." I may not know, but God knows, and just like He said to the man who had been there at the pool with this infirmity for 38 years to get up, *"Take up your bed, and walk"* (John 5:8), God is saying to you, "You have been here too long; get up, take up your bed, and walk into your purpose!" God will send people to hold up your arms when you're weak and tired and when the battle gets hard, just like He did for Moses in Exodus 17:12. *"When Moses' hands grew tired, he could no longer hold them up. So, Aaron and Hur found a stone for him to sit on. Then they stood on each side of Moses, holding up his hands. So, his hands held steady until sunset."*

You're not here by accident; your life has purpose! I believe you are grabbing these truths and your life will never be the same, in Jesus' Mighty name!

Chapter 9

A BLESSING IN THE MIDDLE OF THE STORM

I started having confidence in my worth and the abilities God had given me. My belief system changed. My emotional state also changed and went from despair, pride, and shame to whom God said I was in Psalm 139:14: *"I will praise thee; for I am fearfully and wonderfully made: marvelous are thy works; and that my soul knoweth right well.* Ephesians 1:18: *"Open the eyes of their hearts, and let the light of Your truth flood in. Shine Your light on the hope You are calling them to embrace. Reveal to them the glorious riches You are preparing as their inheritance."*

My path became clearer to me, and the Lord began healing my heart, taking the insecurities away, showing me that if I delight myself in Him, He would give me the desires of my heart (Psalm 37:4).

I so longed to have a husband who would love me the way Christ loved the church and gave himself for it (Ephesians 5:25). God said I needed to be satisfied with Him alone and be completely whole in Him before He would bring my God-fearing husband.

God began preparing me for marriage. I felt like Esther. I started going through the purification process

(Esther 2:12). God wanted to purify my spirit, soul, and body. God wanted me healed and whole (Jeremiah 8:22). The balm in Gilead is a metaphor for the only One who can save us from a disastrous fate. The healing balm — an all-powerful healing balm that would be the only thing to save an incurable condition — that balm is the sacrificial love, death, and resurrection of Jesus Christ our Lord. John 3:16: *"For God so loved the world that he gave his one and only Son, that whoever believes in him shall not perish but have eternal life."*

I began to pray, Lord, *"Create in me a clean heart and renew a steadfast spirit within me"* (Psalm 51:10). I received a word from the Lord saying, "Your husband will find you in the things of the Lord." What was God saying to me? Keep your eyes on Me, follow Me, and I will do the rest. I put myself on the altar of God. The healing and deliverance did come through surrender and humility. Hallelujah!

I was working a full-time job during the day, going to school two nights a week, and braiding hair on the side to make ends meet. I taught on Sundays at church. The requirements of that were that I had to attend the 8am service and then teach my Sunday School class at 11am. I also was heavily involved in the women's ministry, as well as a greeter at church, all of which required monthly meetings. I also attended prayer meetings and Bible study weekly.

I am mentioning my schedule for a reason. Now, if you look at my schedule, where did my children fit into this? My children do have the testimony of being dragged to church, but who was nurturing them and teaching them when I was at school at night, braiding hair, or at ministry meetings? I was so busy trying to fix me, trying to get myself healed and delivered while establishing a career and ministry that I forgot about my children. They had gone through the trauma and abuse right along with me. One of the things that left me with regrets was my pride. I was so in a rush to get a job and get off welfare that I rushed God's plan in the process. Proverbs 16:18 says, *"Pride goeth before destruction, and a haughty spirit before a fall."*

If I could do things differently, I would have just focused on my children and gone to school during the hours they were in school. I would not have been involved in so much ministry because my children needed me to be there for them. I soon learned a very hard lesson: if you are not there to teach and nurture your children and help them through the trials of life, they will turn to sex, drugs, friends, and/or gangs to teach them and comfort them. You could be doing a God thing, but it may not be the right thing or the right time. I should have gotten God's wisdom on this (James 1:5).

God's wisdom equips us to handle difficult situations. There was nothing wrong with my wanting to work and get off welfare. The problem was using wisdom in the timing and process (see Ecclesiastes 10:10). Those who have God's wisdom will show it in the way they live. Every day we have choices to make, and each choice has a consequence or result. If we would all be honest, given the opportunity, we would have made different choices somewhere in our lives, and this was definitely one of them for me. But one thing is for certain: we can learn from our choices by the consequences we experience. It's called the school of hard knocks. My dad used to say a hard head makes for a soft fanny. Hebrews 12:6 says, *"For the Lord disciplines the one He loves and chastens everyone he accepts as his son."*

God was sending messengers to me to tell me to slow down. You're at church too much. Your children should not be left alone in the evenings; they are at crucial ages. I always justified it by saying I am only at school two nights a week, church two nights a week, and the meetings once a month; that's not a lot. That "only" gave me some very hard consequences. I remember the children's grandmother would warn me to be careful about leaving them alone. Proverbs 4:6-7 says, *"Do not forsake wisdom, and she will protect you; love her, and she will watch over you."*

Everything my younger son, Daniel, experienced in the womb — the anger, rage, rejection, and abandonment — was now being acted out. When he was 5 years old his teacher told me she saw something alarming in his behavior. She said, "Your son has a lot of anger in him. I give him a variety of colors to color with, but he always chooses black and red." She told me this was a sign of anger inside. Well, I blew it off and didn't pay much attention to it, until one day another child called him Blacky, and he started beating the little boy's head on the ground. They had a hard time stopping him and getting him to calm down. The teachers all told me my son was very sweet, loving, and kind. He didn't instigate the fights, but he couldn't control his anger once someone pushed his buttons. They suggested I get him some help working through those emotions of anger and rage, which once again I ignored. I was still too busy trying to fill my pain, my voids, and my emptiness.

My older son, Solomon, was starting to have sex and had his first child at 16 years old. Daniel was now 11 years old and starting to hang out with the wrong crowd and was getting into a lot of trouble. He was constantly getting into fights at school. The principal was hesitant in telling me because, remember, I was a volunteer at the school, but she knew things were getting out of control, so she had to bring me into the office and discuss them with me. I tried all kinds of different strategies to turn his behavior around, but nothing was working.

Daniel had his first run-in with the law at age 11. He got into a fight after school with an older kid from a middle school in the area. The kid was getting the best of him, so he picked up a little wooden bat and hit him. The child's parents called the police and the next thing I know they were knocking on my door, telling me the child was ok but that his parents pressed charges and my son must go to court. This happened just when I thought my life was getting on track. I was serving the Lord, I was working in my God-given call, and I was attending college. 1 Peter 1:7 says, *"These trials will show that your faith is genuine. It is being tested as fire tests and purifies gold- though your faith is far more precious than mere gold. So, when your faith remains strong through many trials, it will bring you much praise and glory and honor on the day when Jesus Christ is revealed to the whole world."* My faith was really being challenged and I knew I couldn't blame it all on the devil. I once again had not heeded the warnings or listened to the many messengers God had sent. These were some of the consequences of my choices.

We went to court and God had mercy on my son. Deuteronomy 4:31: "For the Lord your God is a merciful God. He will not leave you or destroy you or forget the covenant with your fathers that he swore to them." The judge dropped the charges because of the child being older and because it was determined that Daniel acted in self-defense. What a sigh of relief!

It didn't stop there, though. Daniel started ditching school and the truant officers came to my house. It was one thing after another. I would be at work, teaching my class, and would get a call that I had to pick up my son from school for one reason or another. Either he was talking back to the teachers, fighting, wearing something outside of the dress code, or not having a belt on and sagging his pants. It eventually got to be too much, so I finished out the semester in college and dropped out so that I could be home in the evenings. With all the fighting and truancies, by the time he was 12 years old, they put him on probation and if he violated his probation, the next step would be juvenile hall for 30 days.

Well, it happened very shortly after that. I will never forget it. It was a summer day, and the boys were out of school. I went to work like any normal day and left him home with his big brother. I received a phone call from Solomon, "Mom, you have to come home. My brother just threw a knife at me." I rushed home and found out that he had asked his brother to do his chores and take out the trash. They started arguing and his brother grabbed a knife and threw it at him. I started disciplining my son and things started getting out of control, so I called the police, but before they could get there he had taken off. I made a police report and of course this was a violation of his parole, so he knew that he would be taken to juvenile hall.

In the middle of all this, God brought my God-fearing husband into my life. My blessing in the middle of the storm came the next day. There was a "suddenly" in my life! I went to go and braid a woman's hair, not thinking that this would be the day I would encounter my husband-to-be. She was also a Christian and we were sharing about the Lord. Her brother, Deno, came downstairs and she introduced him. I noticed that he stayed downstairs, just listening to our conversation. Remember, the Lord had told me my husband would find me in the things of the Lord. He later told me when we started dating that when I was talking to his sister, he saw my love for the Lord was genuine and it attracted him to me.

His older brother, Darius, stopped by. They asked me if I wanted something to eat and I said yes. The next thing I know they invited me on a hike. In that moment I knew I was standing in front of my husband; my spirit was leaping. I began to ask God which one is it? They were both believers, polite, successful gentlemen, and I didn't want to make a mistake and say yes to dating the wrong one. I had already gone down that road with my first husband and rejected the prophecy of the Lord. 1 Thessalonians 5:20 says, *"Do not despise prophetic utterances."* They were so different from all the bad boys in my past.

We went on the hike and Darius was walking next to me on the hiking trail, talking about the Lord and quoting scripture. Deno was trailing behind us with his headphones on, listening to music. I asked God, "Which one is my husband? How will I know?" and He said, "It is not the one doing all the talking and quoting scripture; it is the quiet, humble one." I began to think maybe I heard wrong because the quiet humble one was not making any advances toward me at all. I asked the Lord to give me another sign that he was the one He had chosen for me. They invited me on several hikes, but the last one was when I received my sign.

We arrived back at their sister's house from the hike, and I received a phone call that the police were at my house, looking for my son to arrest him for the knife incident with his brother. I was very upset and couldn't fight back the tears. They both asked me what was wrong, and I began to tell them. They said, "Let us pray for you." This was a blessing to me because no man in my past had ever prayed with me. We held hands in a circle, and they prayed. When the prayer was over, Darius said, "Here, take my card and call me if you need anything." Deno snatched the card out of his hand before I could grab it and said, "What does she need to call you for? She can call me." Boom! There it was — my sign from the Lord. He staked his claim for me. It pays to listen to the Holy Spirit, who will lead us and guide us into all truth (John 16:13). It is so important to let the Lord choose your mate and prepare you for your mate as well. I was always told I would marry a pastor, which neither of them was at the time. But if I were to choose on my own, I would have chosen the one quoting scripture, and that would have been a HUGE mistake.

During my preparation season, the Lord was telling me I needed to have my closets organized and make my bed every day because my husband would be very neat and organized. There had been times when I would be running late for work and leave in a rush and not make my bed and let my closets get all unorganized. Well can I tell you I am glad I listened to God, because that is exactly how my husband is. It saved me from getting into arguments about the house because I was already in a routine of keeping things neat and organized when I met him. God wants to spare us from unnecessary strife.

Deno and I dated for a year and then got married. He chose to help me with my son through good and bad, but he didn't realize how bad bad would get. The pent-up anger and rage that I had ignored was now manifesting.

I want to spend some time talking to you about consequences of ignoring warning signs. What you ignore never gets healed. It just escalates. It won't just go away. They won't just grow out of it. I didn't deal with the root cause of my son's anger and rage, which was stemming from rejection, abandonment, and violence. When you don't allow God to bring healing and deliverance in these areas, it becomes an open door for the enemy to wreak havoc. Ephesians 4:27 says, *"And do not give the devil a foothold."* Jesus' ministry was and is all about bringing healing and deliverance. Matthew 8:16: *"When evening came, they brought to Him many who were demon-possessed; and He cast out the spirits with a word and healed all who were ill."*

I wish I had known then about generational curses. I could have been breaking them off my bloodline, but we will discuss this more in a later chapter. It is your turn now to learn from the choices and consequences that you have brought on yourself or that someone else caused you to have to endure the pain as consequences for their poor choices. You see, both my sons had to endure pain and suffering because of my bad choices. I have learned some valuable lessons and my life has turned around. I had to realize I did the best I knew how to do with what I had been taught.

One thing I want you to stop doing is living a life with regrets. This can be damaging. Regrets not only affect your mind and body, but will keep you from moving forward and becoming fruitful. I had to come to terms with my poor decisions and ask my sons to forgive me and then give myself grace because God gives us grace. Lamentations 3:22-23: *"The steadfast love of the Lord never ceases, his mercies never come to an end; they are new every morning; great is your faithfulness."* You need to give yourself grace, you must realize that sometimes we just didn't have the right tools, the right mindset, or emotional state at the time we made those choices. If you have given your life to the Lord, you now have the mind of Christ and the fruit of the Spirit to help you make better choices. 2 Corinthians 5:17 says, *"Therefore if anyone is in Christ, he is a new creature; the old things are passed away."*

If you haven't given your life to the Lord, take a moment right now and ask Him to come into your heart and be Lord over your life. It's time to allow the blood that Jesus shed for you on Calvary's cross to wash away your sins and wash away those regrets. Isaiah 1:18: *"Come now, and let us reason together, saith the Lord: though your sins be as scarlet, they shall be as white as snow; though they be red like crimson, they shall be as wool."* Forgiveness is yours for the asking! 1 John 1:9: *"If we confess our sins, he is faithful and just to forgive us our sins and to cleanse us from all unrighteousness.*" The devil has had you down much too long; it's time for your "suddenly!"

A Blessing in the Middle of the Storm

Chapter 10

AUTHORITY

I was not expecting what was about to knock the wind out of me and turn my life upside down. Sometimes we know the authority that Jesus has given us in His name, but what will we do when it is time to actually have to exercise it. Philippians 2:9-12 says, *"Therefore, God exalted him to the highest place and gave him the name that is above every name, that at the name of Jesus every knee will bow, in heaven and on earth and under the earth, and every tongue acknowledges that Jesus Christ is Lord, to the glory of God the Father."* We have authority because of the blood of Jesus. The only way to deal with the lies and assaults of Satan is to know your position in the blood of Jesus Christ. The blood that Jesus shed for us on Calvary has the power to save, sanctify, justify, redeem, restore, heal, and deliver.

We often make light of the power in the blood of Jesus, also the tests and trials that God has brought us through. We often keep it to ourselves, but God says in Revelation 12:11, *"And they overcame him by the Blood of the Lamb and the word of their testimony; and they loved not their lives unto the death."* I am reminded of a song that I learned when I first gave my life to Christ, "The Blood That

Jesus Shed for Me." That powerful blood, giving me all of the strength I need, never loses its power. I would not only have to cling to the blood-stained banner like my life depended on it, which it did, but I would have to hold it up. Galatians 6:17: *"From now on let no one trouble me, for I bear in my body the marks of the Lord Jesus."* The idea of "bear" is to undergo experiences that mark one as the slave of some master. The principle: We as believers should carry the mark of belonging to Christ.

How do we apply this to our lives? We who take a stand for the grace principle of the cross will pay a price. We must count the cost. Luke 14:28: *"For which of you, desiring to build a tower, does not first sit down and count the cost, whether he has enough to complete it?"* I was about to find out if I had enough.

I had been going to my sister-in-law's prayer group on Saturdays; they began to teach on spiritual warfare. I began walking out the scripture in Matthew 28:18-20: *"And again He said: 'And these signs will follow those that believe: In My name they will cast out demons; they will speak with new tongues; they will take up serpents; and if they drink anything deadly, it will by no means hurt them; they will lay hands on the sick, and they will recover."* My children would witness me casting demons out of people who came to our house for prayer.

Daniel, with whom I was having problems, was filled with the Holy Spirit. When he was in the 7th grade, he began to exercise his authority in Jesus Christ. One day while he was at school, he was fed up watching the devil have a hold on this one girl who always dressed in all black and seemed to be full of gothic ideas. He started speaking in tongues and casting demons out. He said she was shaking uncontrollably as the demons were coming out. From that day forward the devil really put out a demonic attack against him. He saw my son as a threat to his kingdom. When you walk in kingdom authority, you become a target for the devil. More about this in a later chapter.

Authority

Chapter 11

PARENTS' TEST

When Solomon was 16, he started talking back to me like a lot of teenagers do at that age. They start testing their parents. I remember he told me his teacher told him he could express his opinions to me. I said, "Yes you can, but in a respectful way."

Solomon and I were having battles; he called the police on me for disciplining him. The police showed up and proceeded to tell me that they could call CPS (Child Protective Services) on me and take me to jail. I told them I am not abusing my son; I am just doing what the Bible says in Proverbs 13:24: *"He that spares the rod hates his son: but he that loves him is diligent to discipline him."* I told them that if I don't discipline him, the law will, somewhere down the road. I pointed to the Bible on my table and said, "This is how I choose to raise my son." They backed off and said, "Let us talk to your son for a minute outside." They came back in and told me they told my son that he should respect his mother. You see, I couldn't back down from the devil. I had to exercise my God-given authority. Jesus will always back His word up. Jeremiah 1:12: *"Then the Lord said to me,*

'You have seen well, for I am watching over my word to perform it.'"

Solomon left home because he wanted to drop out of school, and I wasn't having it. I said you will not live under my roof and be a dropout. Well, he was defiant and didn't want to follow my rules, so I told him he had to move out. His grandmother took him in and from there he enlisted in the military. What the devil meant for evil God turned around for his good (see Romans 8:28). He learned a lot of valuable lessons in the military, and he matured really fast.

However, when he got out of the military, he hooked up with a couple of young men whom I could clearly see were up to no good. He had his own apartment and I told him, "Son, they are not good for you; they are going to lead you down the wrong road." I reminded him of the word in 1 Corinthians 15:33: *"Do not be deceived: Bad company corrupts good character."*

One night I received a collect call from the Los Angeles County jail; it was Solomon. He said, "Mom, I need you to get me a lawyer. They have me in custody for attempted robbery." Low and behold, it was the same young men I warned him about. They had robbed a hotel and the police picked my son up right along with them. My son was afraid. He said he was facing a 7 years to life sentence. He begged me to get an attorney for him and I kept telling him,

"God is your attorney." Lamentations 3:58-62: *"Lord, you are my lawyer! Plead my case! For you have redeemed my life. You have seen the wrong they have done to me, Lord. Be my judge and prove me right. You have seen the vengeful plots my enemies have laid against me. Lord, you have heard the vile names they call me. You know all about the plans they have made. My enemies whisper and mutter as they plot against me all day long."* You will soon see how this scripture played out in the court room.

I told my son, "You're going to have to go to Jesus for yourself." He had watched me live a life of fasting and praying. He had watched God come through for me every time. He started fasting and praying behind those bars.

The prosecuting attorneys said they had his fingerprints, but when the judge asked for the evidence to present to the court, they asked for more time. The third time we went to court, the judge told them, "This is the last opportunity you have to present the evidence. If not, I will have to drop all the charges and release him."

God had me hidden in the courtroom. I was sitting where the witnesses normally sit, and they didn't detect me there until I had already heard the prosecuting attorneys talking. One of the attorneys said, "I thought you had his fingerprints?" The other said, "No, I thought I did, but they don't match. How can we get his fingerprints?" "We must go back to the holding tank and get him to give us his fingerprints." They were plotting evil, but God says in Psalm 21:11, *"Though they plot evil against you and devise wicked schemes, they cannot succeed."* When I heard this, I started praying in the spirit real hard and then the bailiff said, "Ma'am, you can't sit there. That is only for witnesses." But by that time, I had already heard what I needed to come up against the devil's wicked schemes. I was reminded of Acts 1:8: *"But you will receive power when the Holy Spirit has come upon you; and you shall be my witnesses in Jerusalem, and in all Judea and Samaria, and to the end of the earth."*

It is important for us to understand just as the Lord wanted the disciples to know that Jesus was not sending them alone or by their own authority to do the work, but that He would still be present in the ministry by His Spirit, and by this they would have the authority to do what He did and say what He said, so that day God brought me in as His witness. Hallelujah! God is amazing! My son had been fasting and praying, so God was working on his behalf. He stood on Psalm 103:10,13: *"He does not deal with us according to our sins; nor repay us according to our iniquities. As a father shows compassion to his children, so the Lord shows compassion to those who fear him."*

Solomon was always a logical thinker and God had given him great wisdom, so when they came to the holding tank, pressuring him to get his fingerprints, he said, "NO, why would I give you, my fingerprints? Supposedly, I was arrested because you said you had my fingerprints." They were telling him he had no other choice but to let them take his fingerprints, and while I was interceding, the bailiff jumped up and went back to the holding tank. He said, "What are you doing? You can't talk to the defendant without his attorney being present." They went back into the courtroom and the judge said, "Do you have the evidence?" They all looked at each other and he said, "Well, do you?" They said, "No," and he said, "Case dismissed."

That was the day Solomon knew that God was his lawyer in the courtroom. He knew that he could go into the courts of heaven and plead his case; he pressed into Jesus for himself. He learned that God's word is true, that there is power in prayer, faith, and trust in Jesus. He also learned a very valuable lesson about the company you keep. He didn't want any part of the prison life. That scared him straight for good, thank you Jesus!

It is very hard for us as mothers to sit back and allow our children to trust Jesus for themselves, and not bail them out every time they get into trouble. They must see God for themselves and have their own testimonies of how God brought them out.

Chapter 12

THE DEVIL'S TARGET

Daniel's rebellion gave the devil an open door. He kept violating his probation, and now, instead of sending him to juvenile hall, they started sending him to camp rehabilitation programs. It was so difficult going through this year after year after year with my son. My husband and I had to face several school boards that wanted to kick him out of their district for fighting or breaking the rules. We were in and out of courts in so many different counties. I don't know how many juvenile detention campsites I had to visit, near and far, from age 12 to 17½.

Remember, I told you I was a volunteer in prison ministry. As a volunteer for the Visto Program for Los Angeles County, I would hold the church services once a month on Sunday mornings, along with a couple of the brothers in the faith. Well, it just so happened that Daniel was transferred to the same camp. Consequently, they had to transfer me to a different camp because it was considered a conflict of interest. No one could have ever told me that my son would end up in the same situation as the young boys I ministered to in the juvenile halls and camps. God has a way of preparing you for things coming up in the future. I had a heart of compassion for these young boys, always trusting and believing that God would turn their lives around. I trusted that God would send someone with the same heart to minister to my son.

It was a long journey. I kept hoping every time Daniel came home from juvenile camp that he would turn his life around. I tried taking him to counseling at the church, also to court-ordered counseling, but he wouldn't open up to anyone. Eventually, the counselors gave up on him and said it was a waste of time; they were not getting anywhere with him. I started feeling at a loss for how to help him, other than praying. I even tried a couple of mentors in the church. I also tried sending him to his uncle's house, thinking another male figure would help, but to no avail. I remembered the scriptures and that is what I held onto: *"Train up a child in the way he should go: and when he is old, he will not depart from it"* (Proverbs 22:6). SHOULD GO are the key words in this scripture. Just because you show them the right road doesn't mean they are going to take it, and only God knows how long before they turn around and utilize the training.

I had received prophetic words over both of my sons, how one was a prophet, and one was a teacher of the Word. I knew that one day they would walk in their calling. I kept speaking what God said about them. I refused to speak death over them. Proverbs 18:21: *"Death and life are in the power of the tongue: and they that love it shall eat the fruit thereof."*

There comes a time when we will be tested and either we give in to the devil or we exercise the authority that God has given us in Luke 10:19. He says, *"I have given you authority to trample on snakes and scorpions and to overcome all the power of the enemy; nothing will harm you."*

Daniel was still in and out of juvenile camp, and this last time they gave him six months to a year, depending on his behavior. He would always blame me for his getting locked up. He would say, "You're always telling my probation officer on me." I knew I would have to use tough love, that lying to keep him out of juvenile hall wouldn't help. It had now been 5 years of the back and forth, so you can only imagine what I was going through emotionally, just trying to keep it all together. I didn't do everything right as a parent, but I would speak life over him and minister to him every time I went to visit him.

This time was the longest he had ever spent in camp. It was almost a year, so I just knew things would be different when he was released this time. He was now 17½. He came home, and it was still more of the same: not following any rules at home, and coming and going as he pleased. I kept believing and trusting God for a change in him, because 1

Thessalonians 2:13 says, *"For this reason we also thank God without ceasing, because, when you received the word of God which you heard from us, you welcomed it not as the word of men, but as it is in truth, the word of God, which also effectively works in you who believe."*

No matter what I did, Daniel wouldn't turn around. One day I lost my cool with him and I made a big mistake and pushed him and told him, "You have caused me nothing but pain ever since you were born." Parents, one thing we should never do is break our child's spirit. We should never discipline when frustrated or angry. I didn't really mean that; remember, I had been speaking life. I allowed the devil to get me to speak death out of frustration, but once the words leave your mouth you can't get them back. James 3:8: *"But the tongue can no man tame; it is an unruly evil, full of deadly poison."* This is why it is dangerous to harbor unforgiveness in your heart. The Bible says in Matthew 15:18, *"But the things that come out of the mouth proceeds from the heart, and these things defile a man."*

I didn't realize that I had a lot of unforgiveness for what he was taking me through. The Bible says, *"For out of the abundance of the heart the mouth speaks"* (Luke 6:45). I had to clean my heart of any unforgiveness because only the Lord knew I had a long journey ahead of me and I would need to keep my heart right in order to endure to the end.

Daniel walked out the door the day I said those words to him; those words cut like a knife.

He went to stay with several family members after he left, but burned his bridges with everyone. He ended up homeless on the streets. He would call me collect in the middle of the night and tell me how cold it was. My heart was just breaking. My friend would give him gift cards so he could get himself something to eat, and she even tried to put him up in a hotel, but he wouldn't go. I didn't understand that, but the reason would soon be revealed.

I received a phone call from an old friend in Baldwin Park who said, "You need to come and pick your son up; something is wrong with him; he is acting very strange." I went to pick him up but by the time I arrived he was gone.

The next time I saw Daniel he was literally out of his mind. He showed up at my doorstep, now 18 years old. When I opened the door, I was in shock. He looked just like the homeless people on the streets. He was dirty and smelled really bad. Both of my sons always had been well kept from head to toe, so I knew something was truly wrong when I saw that he had on pants that were too small, with white gym socks and dress shoes, and his hair was unkempt. This was totally out of character for him.

He came inside and I observed the same strange behavior that my neighbor had witnessed prior to calling me.

He went into the kitchen to make himself something to eat and then looked at me and started cussing in Spanish. Now mind you, Daniel was rebellious, but he had never disrespected me with his words — only his behavior. So, I knew he definitely wasn't in his right mind.

Deno and I would be asleep at night, and we would hear him reading the back of the cereal box out loud and blasting his TV as if he was trying to drown out the demonic voices he was hearing. I took him to an intercessory prayer group I belonged to, and we all prayed for him, but there was no change.

One day he snapped back for a moment into reality. How do I know this? Because I knew my child and I knew when he was talking and when the demons were talking. He started gagging, saying, "Mom, God made Adam and Eve, not Adam and Steve." He said that he was cold and hungry on the streets and this man offered to put him up in a hotel and told him he would give him a job to help him get on his feet. When he went to sleep the man came in the room and started trying to force his tongue in his mouth and he had to fight him off. Thank God Daniel was able to fight him off, but what a traumatic experience, so hard for me to even imagine. The more he talked about it the more he gagged. Then he slipped back out of reality and went into his room and started blasting the Trinity Broadcasting Network (TBN) on television, the Christian Word Network, as if to drown out that memory.

Deno was saying he needs to be in a controlled environment; this is not safe. I kept saying we have to help him. It seems like when the child that you carried in your womb and birthed is going through a hard time, it is hard for you to reason, and your emotions take over. We looked up Christian men's homes, but when we would arrive, because of his strange behavior, they would ask us if he was on meds. We would tell them, "No, he just ended up on our doorstep like this," and they would refuse to take him.

One night he left the house, and in the middle of the night I received a call from the police, saying, "Can you come and pick up your son? We have him here because he was trying to get on a bus with no shirt, no socks, and no shoes. I don't want to put him back out on the streets like this." For the life of me, I don't know what happened to the clothes and shoes my husband had given him to wear.

I woke Deno up. He was not happy at all, but he drove me down to the jail to pick him up. This was putting a real strain on our marriage, so I was fighting multiple battles at one time. This all happened in the span of two weeks.

I was fasting, praying, worshipping, and pressing into God more than ever. I would walk the floors in the middle of the night, speaking in my heavenly language, and declaring

103

and decreeing what God had spoken over my son. I also had to do the same for my husband because he said he couldn't take it anymore with Daniel, and he wanted a divorce. I had to stand in my authority, and on the word of God. I told him, "You are not going anywhere. I am the blessed woman whom God gave you." No matter how he responded, I kept speaking the Word. I knew the Word carried weight. He went so far as to hire a paralegal to draw up divorce papers, but God's word prevailed!

I felt like I was in the fight of my life. One night I was crying out to God, saying, "I don't know what to do, Lord. How do I help my son?" My son was up as usual, blasting the TV in the middle of the night. I said, "Come on, let's go to the hospital. Daniel, are you on any drugs? He said, "No, Mom. I told you I am not taking anything." The Lord dropped in my spirit this mental hospital that I would always pass, that was on a main vein in my area. So, I drove him to Canyon Ridge Mental Hospital.

When we arrived, I spoke to the intake nurse and told him what I was experiencing with my son. He asked how old he was, and when I said 18, he said, "Because he is 18, we can't evaluate him or even admit him unless he consents to it." I asked, "If he is not in his right mind, how would he know he needs help?" I was crying, desperate for answers. God moved on the man's heart, and he said, "Ok, if you take your son to Chino Valley Community Hospital and have them check him for any drugs in his system, and then bring the results to us, we will evaluate him (see Proverbs 21:1). We know that God has the power to change the hearts of men. I was so relieved. I had seen God moving.

I drove to the hospital and encountered the same thing. He is 18 so you cannot come into the room with him. I told the nurse he was not in his right mind, and she said that rules are rules.

She took Daniel back into the room, and within minutes she said, "Can you come back to the room with him?" She was uncomfortable with his behavior. I said, "I tried to tell you." They took his blood work, and while we were waiting, he kept repeating to me, "Mom, I am not on drugs." The test results came back negative for drugs, so we drove back to Canyon Ridge for the evaluation.

They took my son in by himself and evaluated him and then they called me in by myself to tell me the results. I was told my son had a mental breakdown; they see this a lot with homeless people. They literally check out in their minds because they cannot deal with the reality of their situation, and the cold and malnutrition doesn't help their mental state at all. They recommended outpatient care and gave me a referral. The doctor told me my son was not a threat to himself or anybody else, and that gave me some peace. The next day I took him to the outpatient clinic. It was overwhelming, being in the waiting room with so many people not in their right mind. Then we went home.

We had been at the hospital the night before until 3am, so I was mentally and emotionally exhausted. I stopped at the mailbox before we went into the house and there was a letter from his grandmother. I said, "Son, your grandmother sent some money so you can buy some new clothes." Remember, he showed up on my doorstep with nothing, and had been borrowing his stepfather's clothes.

I told him I was going to take a nap before Bible study. I grabbed a blanket and laid down on my bed. I had peace going to sleep because the doctor's last words to me were, "YOUR SON IS NOT A THREAT TO HIMSELF OR ANYBODY ELSE." We should never take man's wisdom over God's because, if you recall, my husband had given me a word from God that he was a threat and needed to be in a controlled environment. 1 Corinthians 2:5 reads, *"That your faith might not stand on the wisdom of men, but on the power of God."* I had trusted the words of the doctor. Only God could have prepared me for what was about to happen next, because the attack that was about to occur would have been worse without the Holy Spirit's leading.

Chapter 13

THE ATTACK

I had taken the money his grandmother sent Daniel out of the envelope and put it in my bra, which was something I had never done before. We had a key holder in our kitchen, and it was our habit to hang the keys on it when we walked in the door. Well, this time I put the keys in my jacket pocket. Within minutes of lying down I heard him in the shower, and I could hear him talking to someone on the phone. I got up and went to the bathroom door and heard him asking his grandmother if she had sent cash or a check. I cracked the bathroom door open, and I said, "You cannot take the phone into the shower. You are going to break it." He said, "What are you trying to do? Come in here and molest me?"

The devil was bringing back to his mind what the man tried to do to him at the hotel. I said, "No," and I shut the door as fast as I could. I went to lie back down and within minutes he was standing over me with a knife and saying in a very demanding, threatening voice, "WHERE'S THE MONEY? GIVE ME THE MONEY." I was hysterical. I was trying to reach for the money in my bra, but I don't think he knew the money was on my person, and because I wasn't getting up, he repeated himself again in an even louder, more demanding and threatening voice, "WHERE'S THE MONEY? GIVE ME THE MONEY." Before I could get it out of my bra, he jabbed me with the knife on my forearm.

I couldn't believe what was happening. You can only imagine if I had not felt led to put all those items on my person, I would have had to get up and would have been wide open to getting stabbed in the back or chest. There is no telling what would have happened. I got the money out and then he said, "WHERE'S THE KEYS? GIVE ME THE KEYS," and before I could get them out of my pocket, he stabbed me with the knife again, this time in my legs and arms because I was trying to defend myself by putting up my arms and legs while trying to get the keys out at the same time. He then said, "WHERE IS MY DAD? GIVE ME MY DAD BACK," and he stabbed me in my private area as if to say I hate that I came out of here.

I knew the devil was talking to him saying, "Kill her. She took your dad from you." I was terrified for my life. He then snatched me up off the bed as if he had superpower strength. I hear when people are out of their mind and their adrenaline is going, they get really strong. I said to myself I am going to die now.

My life flashed before my eyes. I began to have a conversation with God, I said, "God, I worship you; I serve you; I give; I help others; and this is how you are going to let me die?" I heard the Lord say, "I gave you everything you need to fight this battle." Instantly, I remembered my authority I had in Jesus' name over the demons that were operating through my son. You see, God is not going to do for us what He has already given us the power to do. My son had the knife in his hand. I pointed in his face and said, "SATAN, IN THE NAME OF JESUS, YOU STOP NOW." Immediately, Daniel stopped and ran out. I hurried up and locked the bedroom door. Then I realized, wait, my bedroom is upstairs. How am I going to get out? I am going to bleed to death. There was so much blood. I am a bleeder, and it looked like a slaughterhouse. I didn't have the phone because remember, he had it in the bathroom. And I didn't own a cellphone. I contemplated jumping out the two-story window, but I heard the Lord say, "He is gone."

I cracked open the bedroom door and called out his name a couple of times. There was no answer. I opened the door, and I could see the front door had been left wide open. So, I ran with all my might to the next-door neighbor's house for help. It was a good thing she kept calm because I was in shock. All I kept saying over and over was that I thought I was going to die, as she grabbed a sheet and ripped off pieces and started trying to stop the bleeding. She called 911 at the same time. When the ambulance arrived, I was still repeating the same thing over and over that I thought I was going to die. They said, "Ma'am, you are safe now. We need you to calm down."

They put me in the ambulance and cut off my clothes so they could see where the bleeding was coming from. It took forever to get to the hospital because it was during heavy traffic hours when people were getting off work. They could not take me to just any hospital. They said they had to take me to a hospital that had a trauma unit.

At the hospital they examined me and told me I had been stabbed eight times, but that none of them penetrated any of my vital organs. God is good and true to His word. He says the weapon will be formed but it won't prosper. Isaiah 54:17: *"No weapon that is formed against thee shall prosper; every tongue that rises against thee in judgement thou shalt condemn. This is the heritage of the servants of the Lord, and their righteousness is of me, saith the Lord."* That day that scripture I had quoted so often in prayer and in ministry came to life for me.

My husband had just gotten a cellphone a couple of days prior and because God blessed me with a photographic memory, I remembered the number, thank the Lord. My husband was working a side job painting homes, so without that cellphone they wouldn't have been able to reach him. When they called him, he went straight to the house to meet with the police. He saw all the blood and said, "My wife cannot come home and see all this blood and relive that nightmare." He cleaned all the blood and shampooed the carpet before coming to the hospital. My family gathered together at the hospital in the waiting room. The doctor came out and gave them the good news that I was going to be alright, and they were going to release me after they ran a couple of tests. I was released within a couple of hours, only by the grace of God!

When I arrived home, I asked God what this was all about. He said, "The devil wanted to kill you, put your son in prison for the rest of his life, and destroy your marriage so the ministry God has for you guys would not go forth." The Lord then said to me, "Tanya, will you let Me get the glory out of you and your son's life? Will you let Me get the glory out of this tragedy?" I said, "Yes Lord, I trust You," and He said, "I know it hurts, but I will heal your broken heart, and deliver and restore your son and your marriage." I said, "Yes Lord." That "Yes Lord" meant that I would not complain or whine about what had happened, but allow God to help others through my tragedy.

My sister called and said Daniel had called her and asked her to bring him gas money, saying he was on his way to Vegas and ran out of gas. My sister knew he had stolen my car, so she stalled him and called the police and told them his location. When the police arrived to arrest him for attempted murder, grand theft auto, and robbery, he didn't even remember what he had done. The arresting officer came to my house, full of compassion for my son, with tears in his eyes. He said, "I hope you get help for your son. He has no idea what he has done. He was really out of it when we arrested him."

My husband was upset, and said, "Tanya, I told you he needed to be in a controlled environment, and you didn't heed the word." God will send His messengers, but it is hard to hear when it is your child. Your emotions get all entangled in the mess. My emotions were so caught up, my armor was down to where I couldn't even cast out the demons like I had cast out of so many others.

The day after the attack, my arm felt so heavy. I told Deno something was wrong. My husband said it was probably just sore because he stabbed me in my muscle. He went off to work but my arm was really bothering me, so I decided to go to the hospital to get this checked out. I drove myself to the hospital. As I was walking down the walkway, a lady came up to me and said, "Can you pray for me? I see a bright light shining over you." I said "Yes." I walked a little further and a man coming out of the hospital asked me to pray for him. I was thinking to myself, I don't have on a cross; I don't have on a Jesus t-shirt, I am not carrying a Bible. Why are they asking me, a stranger, to pray for them?

Quickly, Psalm 34:18 came to me: *"The Lord is close to the brokenhearted and saves those who are crushed in spirit."* I knew that the light they had seen over me was because God was carrying me through this storm.

The doctor ordered x-rays to be taken of my arm. The x-rays showed that blood was built up inside my arm and it had caused an infection. That was the worst of my physical injuries, and all I can do is say thank You, Jesus. You truly do mean what You say in Psalm 91:1-6: *"He who dwells in the secret place of the Most High God shall abide under the shadow of the Almighty. I will say of the Lord, He is my refuge and fortress: my God; in him will I trust. Surely, he shall deliver thee from the snare of the fowler, and from the noisome pestilence. He shall cover thee with his feathers, and under his wings shalt thou trust: his truth shall be thy shield and buckler. Thou shalt not be afraid for the terror by night; nor for the arrow that flieth by day; Nor for the pestilence that walketh in darkness; nor for the destruction that wasteth at noonday."* I would run into the secret place, literally, over that two-week span that I was trying to get help for Daniel. I would put on my worship music and cover my head and say, "Lord, hide me." The Lord means it when He says he who dwells in the secret place, and boy, did He protect me from the destruction that came in the noonday.

The Attack

Chapter 14

FORGIVENESS

I survived the attack, but I still would have a long journey ahead of me. The next 9 months would seem like I was carrying a baby. I was awaiting the deliverance and new birth for my youngest son, Daniel, who was now facing three charges — one for attempted murder, robbery, and grand theft auto. They also combined his past record from juvenile hall and gang affiliation, which they would later use against him to add to his sentence.

I made phone calls to find out what jail they had taken Daniel to. I then made an appointment to visit him. It was terrifying walking alone down the corridors through the cemented walls. I was so afraid that a stranger was going to come around that corner at any time. You could literally feel a demonic presence in those corridors. I said, "Lord, cover me with Your blood and send Your angels of protection."

When I arrived at his unit, I had to pick up the phone and let the guard know whom I was there to visit. He told me to hold on while they informed Daniel that he had a visitor. The guard came back and told me, "I'm so sorry. Your son refused the visit." I left there crying and very saddened. I didn't know what to think, or what was in his mind. I cried out to the Lord, "Lord, you healed the lunatic in the Bible who had legions of demons in him, so you can deliver, heal, and restore my son's mind," (see Mark 5:1-7). I knew it was not my son who was acting out, but the demons that were tormenting and oppressing him. I said, "Lord, all I want is his mind back." I said, "Devil, THIS MEANS WAR."

I began to do spiritual warfare for my son's mind. I called all my prayer warriors, and I even sent a prayer request into TBN, along with my son's picture. I made another appointment to go and visit my son, but to no avail. He refused the visit again, but I refused to give up. I made another appointment, and this time he accepted the visit. God answers prayers.

They had my son on the ward with all the other inmates who were out of their minds. They were wearing a different color from the other inmates. When I arrived, they had me sit down at the window and pick up the phone. They brought Daniel out in shackles on his wrists and ankles. They put him in a closed, locked room that had a small opening in it. They then had him put his wrists in the hole and they unlocked the shackles off his wrists. He looked very despondent, and couldn't look me in my eyes. I noticed his lips were really swollen and puffy like he had an allergic reaction to something. I was so mad at the devil that I said, "You are going to pay for this. Every time I come here; I am going to speak deliverance over all the inmates that I come in contact with." I did just that. I spoke deliverance prayers over them and encouraged their families to stand and believe for their deliverance.

I asked Daniel if he remembered what had happened the day of the stabbing, and he put his head down and said, "Yes, Mom, and I asked the Lord to forgive me." I could see my son had remorse and conviction, but that he also was wearing shame and guilt. We know that shame and guilt does not come from God but from the evil one. It is one thing to be remorseful over your mistakes, but it is another thing to walk in guilt and condemnation. In Romans 7:24, Paul writes about his hatred over his sinful nature that continues to war against his new nature in Christ. He is showing remorse over his sin, he hates the sin, but he knows that he has been set free from the bondage of sin and slavery. In Romans 8:2, Paul tells us that we are free from feelings of condemnation, which means that the law no longer has the power to condemn us because we are not under the law but under grace. When we ask God for forgiveness, He says He has compassion on us and throws our sins into the depths of the sea (see Micah 7:19).

I also needed to let Daniel know I forgave him. I said, "Son, I forgive you for what you did. I know it was not you who attacked me, but the demons that were operating

117

through you. The devil was out to take your mind and lock you up in prison for the rest of your life because you are a threat to his kingdom, but God said not so in 2 Corinthians 2:14: '*Now thanks be unto God, which always causes us to triumph in Christ, and makes manifest the savor of his knowledge by us in every place.*'" He then told me, "Mom, they had me on some medication, but the Lord told me to stop taking it, that it was harming me and not helping me."

During the next 9 months, every time I went to visit, I could see the Lord's healing hand upon him. I could see him coming more and more back to the son I knew before the demonic attack.

Chapter 15

DELIVERANCE IN THE MIDST OF CONSEQUENCES

By the end of 9 months I could see the complete healing. God restored Daniel's mind. My son came running out for our visit without the shackles on his hands or ankles. He said, "Mom, look! I am free from the chains! And look, Mom, they changed the color of clothes I wear! MOM, I AM NOT CRAZY!"

I was reminded of Lazarus in John 11:42, 43: *"I knew that you always hear me, but I said this for the benefit of the people standing here, that they may believe that you sent me."* When he had said this, Jesus called in a loud voice, *'Lazarus. Come out!'* The dead man came out, his hands and feet wrapped with strips of linen, and cloth around his face. Jesus said to them, *"Take off the grave clothes and let him go."* God said, "Take those grave clothes off Daniel and let his mind go and let him out of that crazy unit." Hallelujah! God took off the grave clothes. I believe what took place prior to them taking off the grave clothes was the way God told the evil spirits to come out of the man with the legions in Mark 5: 8-9: *"For he said unto him, 'Come out of the man, thou unclean spirit.' And he asked him, 'What is thy name?' And he answered, saying, 'My name is Legion: for we are*

119

many.'" You really see the victory in verse 15*: "And then they saw him sitting there, dressed and in his right mind; and they were afraid."*

The court ordered Daniel to be sent to Patton State Hospital for a 90-day evaluation of his mental state. During his time there, I was able to visit him without the glass between us. I was able to actually lay hands on my son and pray for him. This again, was a very demonic environment. Daniel would tell me of people screaming all hours of the night, being tormented by the devil.

The time came for Daniel to get prepared to go to court. They gave him a public defender, who was trying to talk him into pleading temporary insanity. Daniel told him, "I will not plead temporary insanity. I will do my time for what I have done because even though I wasn't in my right mind when it happened, it was my disobedience and rebellion that brought me to this point." The public defender was very angry, and he told me, "You need to talk to your son. I could get him off with little or no prison time if he pleads temporary insanity."

What he didn't know was that I had already prayed and said, "God, you know how much time my son needs, and I don't want him out a minute too soon or a minute too late. Lord, not my will, but your will be done." Jesus prayed in Luke 22:42, *"Father, if you are willing, remove this cup from me: nevertheless, not my will, but thine be done."* I said, "Lord, put it in Daniel's heart how You want him to plead to the charges."

I told the public defender, "I will not try to convince my son to plead temporary insanity. Whatever he told you is what the Lord has put in his heart." The public defender was so mad he slammed out of the room and said, "Something is wrong with you and your son. He doesn't have to do time in prison."

When it came time for my son to plead, they presented a plea bargain to him. They said, "If you plead guilty to the greater charge of attempted murder, we will drop the other two lesser charges. My son agreed, signed the plea bargain, and pleaded guilty to attempted murder.

I was walking this journey alone with just me, God the Father, God the Son, and God the Holy Spirit. It was a very tough time. I felt all alone; I had nothing left but to hold on to the blood-stained banner of Jesus Christ to cover me and carry me through like He had done throughout all the other trials in my life. The blood of Jesus has never failed me!

My husband, Deno, was still fighting unforgiveness, and if I even mentioned Daniel's name, his whole body language would be that of anger and disgust. You see, prior to the attack, Deno had poured so much into Daniel, trying to be the best stepfather he could be in the midst of every trial and storm he went through with him. This was like the straw that broke the camel's back for him. Deno would say, "I almost lost my wife," and it took him a very long time to get past it. He was stuck in the "What if he had killed my wife? What if she was paralyzed? What if she is emotionally messed up?"

My family and friends never offered to go to court with me or even to go visit my son with me. I believe God purposed it that way because some things God just wants you to walk through the trials of life alone so that nobody gets the credit for carrying you and bringing you out but Him.

It was time for my son to stand before the judge. My heart was beating so fast I thought it was going to pop out of my chest as I sat in the courtroom. The first thing the judge told my son is that she was proud of him for not trying to get out of his punishment by pleading temporary insanity. She said, "I have read your report from the psychological evaluation and Daniel, you are not crazy, but if you had pleaded temporary insanity to get out of serving jail time, you would have been crazy by the time you got out of that place." I knew the Lord was speaking through the judge to speak over the lies of the devil. The judge said, "I am going to try to get you less time for owning your mistakes." The judge gave him 12 years and said he would have to serve 85%

of that time due to the prior record and gang affiliation. They call these enhancements to your charges. I was not prepared to hear 12 years. I don't know how many years I thought they would give him because I never put a number in my mind, but I definitely wasn't ready for that.

They took my son out of the court room and to this day I couldn't tell you how I made it to my car or even how I made it home, for that matter. I cried so hard until I couldn't cry anymore. I was screaming saying, "NO GOD, NO," over and over, all the way home. Then I was reminded of when God had said, "Tanya, will you let Me get the glory out of you and your son's life" and I said, "Yes Lord," but I didn't know it would be this hard. He said, "Tanya, I will strengthen you every step of the way."

Daniel was always in prisons where I would have to travel at least 3 to 4 hours to see him. God began to work on Deno's heart. He didn't visit with me but would drive me to the many prisons that Daniel was in. It took several years, but my husband was finally able to have full forgiveness and it was no longer his stepson; he considered him his son. God made the relationship better than before. Malachi 4:6 says, *"And he shall turn the heart of the fathers to the children, and the heart of the children to their parents."*

The next 11½ years would be very trying. It was like I was being punished along with my son, with all the rules of visiting that change from prison to prison. They treat you like a criminal when you visit an inmate, and make you feel less than a human being. However, God did get the glory out of this very tragic situation.

I was catapulted into the ministry. God put it on a great man and woman of faith, the late Pastor Alexander Huizar and his beautiful wife, Pastor Janice Huizar, to have me come to their TV ministry called "Jesus Cares for You Ministry." They had faith like I had never seen before. I can still hear him speaking to me now, encouraging me saying, "HALLELUJAH PRAISE THE LORD, WOMAN OF GOD. STEP OUT IN FAITH; THERE IS NOTHING GOD CANNOT DO." I was asked to share my testimony about my son Daniel and to minister in dance on the broadcast. The Lord soon told them to ordain me as an evangelist and I began to see how the Lord was using this testimony to bless others and bring healing and deliverance.

The song I used to minister in dance was "In the Secret Place," by Karen Clark Sheard. This was my go-to song over those two weeks when Daniel showed up at my doorstep out of his mind. Remember how I shared with you in an earlier chapter how I would run into His presence and say, "Lord, hide me in your secret place; hide me in your tabernacle." I was asked to speak at my church for the women's ministry. My first sermon was "Pressing Through the Pain," in which I ministered about standing firm in faith and allowing God to get the glory out of your pain. It was literally a pressing into God for me in order to make it through this very long chapter of my life.

I went back into the juvenile halls and camps with the testimony of my son Daniel. I would share with young men from the ages of 12 to 18, and I would tell them how rebellion, disobedience, gangs, drugs, and alcohol could cause them to wake up one day facing some serious prison charges. I said sin and rebellion will take you farther than you ever could have imagined, and you will wake up asking "How did I get here?" I know my son never thought that he would wake up one day behind prison bars, facing attempted murder charges against his own mother.

Most of these young men were from broken homes where the fathers were absent and all they had were their mothers, so they had a lot of compassion for me. I would see some really hardened and hardcore gang members be humbled and brought to tears by my testimony. God was bringing healing to me at the same time, and the inmates would encourage me and say, "I will be praying for you and your son." What blessed them so much was that I told them I had forgiven my son and still believed God had a great plan for his life, and every word spoken over my son by the Lord would one day come to pass, no matter what it looked like.

Chapter 16

NOT OVER YET

Daniel's prison term was finally up, and he was released on 3 years of parole. They didn't allow him to parole to my house because they said I was the victim of the crime. He would not be able to have any contact with me for the 3 years until his parole was up. You want to talk about another blow from the devil. Here I am waiting for 11½ years for my son to be released so I could finally hold him in my arms and the devil says, "Sike... You still can't have him back." My heart was crushed, but God opened a door for him to parole to his half-brother, Michael's house. This was the son his father, Vance, had with Rhonda. God was working in his life. He started working construction with his brother.

Daniel had been out of prison for a year, and I was overjoyed to hear how well he was doing. One day I received the news of trouble in paradise. The waters were being troubled. His brother, Michael, started having some relationship problems and told Daniel he was going to have to move. They ended up moving, but then Daniel was told they would have to move again, so Daniel ended up on his older brother Solomon's doorstep. He stayed for a couple of days, but Solomon's wife said he couldn't live there, so he felt rejected and abandoned once again.

I didn't blame Solomon's wife. She didn't know him and had only heard the story of what had happened between us. His grandmother connected him with his biological father, Vance, with whom he had never had a relationship. His father told him he had a backhouse for him to stay in and he would help him get back on his feet. Daniel's older brother, Solomon, told him, "That is not a good idea for you to go with dad. Nothing good is going to come out of that." Solomon also told me, "Mom, it is not a good idea for Daniel to go with our dad; please talk to him. My dad is still messed up."

You see, when he left me for Rhonda they got strung out on some really bad drugs. He was no longer with Rhonda and was with another woman. I worked around the corner from Rhonda's house and God had put it on my heart to pray for her, so I had begun going on my lunch break to pray for her to be saved and get delivered from the drugs. Now remember, God had given my son, Solomon, great wisdom, but I said, "If he wants to get to know his dad, who are we to stop him?" He said, "Ok Mom. Don't say I didn't warn you."

Daniel made his way to his father's house, and started immediately looking for work. He didn't have a copy of his social security card because it got lost somewhere while moving from place to place. His dad wasn't working. Only his girlfriend worked. He stayed home all day, drinking and getting high. He began harassing Daniel to hurry up and get a job because, he said, "You can't live here for free." He had reneged on what he had told him prior to coming, that he didn't have to pay rent. He was really just trying to take some heat off himself because his girlfriend had been harassing him to get a job.

One day he knocked on Daniel's door and got in his face, cussing at him and degrading him. Daniel knew that he had to get out of there before he caught another case. You see, there had still been no breaking of the generational curses, so it was the big hulk with anger and rage meeting little hulk with anger and rage. Daniel was on parole, so he called his parole officer and told her he was now homeless. She recommended a men's home close by his father's house. Daniel arrived there and kept calling his dad to bring him his clothes and some hygiene products. His dad never showed up, and the men soon started talking about how bad he smelled.

Daniel was frustrated, hurt, and angry, so he left the men's home and took off to an old friend's house in Orange County. He crashed on his friend's sofa for a couple of days and then decided to make his way back to Solomon's house. While at the bus stop, he ran into trouble with someone who was high on drugs and kept coming toward him. He kept telling the guy to back off. The guy lunged toward him and before you knew it, all the anger and rage he had for his dad and his situation came out on the guy. Daniel was missing for two weeks. Nobody knew where he was. His phone was going straight to voicemail.

I received a phone call at work, and I hit the floor. I felt like the devil had sucker-punched me. I was devastated when I heard Daniel was back in prison. I just knew that after serving all that time that that was the end of it. He had been out for a year and was doing so well. Don't ever lay down your weapons. The devil is just waiting to catch you off guard.

I started studying up on generational curses and you had better believe it that after this, Vance's mom and I have broken those generational curses. They didn't consider it self-defense and Daniel caught another assault case. They gave him 6½ years because, of course, they used his priors against him.

Daniel ended up serving 6 years of the sentence. I didn't think I could muster up the strength to go through this again. That's why the Bible says, *"The race is not given to the swift nor the battle to the strong but those that endure to the end* (Ecclesiastes 9:11). The thought of going back and forth to court again and traveling to visit him at different prisons made me sick to my stomach. I was crying, saying to myself, "When will we get over the rainbow?" In other words, when will God's promise be fulfilled in Daniel. I was reminded by God again. I heard Him saying, "Tanya, will you allow Me to get the glory out of this?" I again said, "Yes, Lord." I would also receive the word over and over, "*To whom much is given much is required*" (Luke 12:48).

So, you may ask, "Where is everyone today? Rhonda was delivered from the hardcore drugs; thank you, Jesus. I am still believing God for her salvation and full deliverance from addictions. I still see Rhonda from time to time at family events with our sons because all three brothers are really close, and Rhonda's son, Michael, is like a son to me. We are still praying and believing for deliverance for their father, Vance.

My husband, Deno, and I went on to serve on the board of directors at the church at which we were serving, and we served many ministries before God had us ordained as pastors 8 years ago. God blessed us to plant our church in Upland, California, where we are honored to still serve today.

Daniel received his G.E.D. while serving the second prison term, and I was overjoyed to be able to attend his cap and gown ceremony. When it was time for Daniel to be released, he had a hearing with the parole board. They asked him whose house to which he was paroling. He told them, "I am paroling to my mom's house," and they said ok, but they set him up. Little did we know that they would put in his release papers that he couldn't have contact with the victim, which we thought was the guy he assaulted and did the time for. As it turned out, it was me.

The next day I took Daniel to the parole department to check in. They asked Daniel how he got down there, and he said, "My mom brought me." The next thing I knew the parole officer walked Daniel out to where I was waiting in the car and asked me to come inside, lying to me by saying the neighborhood was not safe for me to be waiting in my car. It was a trap to get me inside with my son, and get my driver's license to prove I was indeed the victim. They then asked me to wait in the waiting room. Within about 15 minutes they told me they were arresting my son for violation of his parole.

Now mind you, Daniel had only been out of prison for 24 hours. I was crying and telling them this was not Daniel's fault because he was not told this by the parole board, and his parole papers did not say Tanya on them. They said he still violated, and were taking him in. This was another big blow from the devil, working through our broken system. The next day I called the supervisor and explained the situation. He said, "I will try and have him released in a couple of days." Can you see how hard the devil was working to keep my son in bondage? I reached out to friends, prayer warriors at our church, and Wailing Wall Ministries, and they started bombarding heaven on my son's behalf. He was finally released after 3 days. They told him the reason he violated was because when he was released the first time for assaulting me that he was only out for a year, and he had 2 more years to not be in contact with the victim, which made no sense because he was in prison, away from me for 6 years. He had already served his time for the assault charges against me. The parole papers should have applied to the guy he got in the fight with that landed him back in prison.

We really need to pray for our justice system. Thanks be to God Daniel has been working and doing well for the past 18 months. We are still believing God for Daniel to walk in his call and purpose that God has intended for his life. We believe Daniel will go back and snatch souls out of the devil's kingdom. God is breaking the social anxiety off him and building his self-confidence. The devil's plan to silence him is broken in Jesus' name! You see, God is a promise keeper. He did and is still getting the glory out of Daniel's and my life! This is nothing we have done, but all that Jesus has done in and through us, God gets all the glory!

We know one day Daniel will tell his own testimony of his journey to freedom. All of us as believers in Jesus

Christ must carry the blood-stained banner of the cross. It will not be the most comfortable or the most popular or pleasing to people, but it will show our faithfulness to God. We should see ourselves as soldiers on the battlefield, people should be able to clearly see the marks of our belonging to Christ.

Galatians 6:17: *"From now on let no one trouble me, for I bear in my body the marks of the Lord Jesus."* The word "marks" is the Greek word, stigma. A stigma was a permanent brand, tattoo, or mark burnt in the skin. Paul gives the Galatians a challenge to look at the price he paid for taking a stand for the cross of Christ. That is the burden Paul bore. He bore or endured the burden of the cross.

You may have or may be going through way worse in your life and you thought by now the mountains would move, by now the chains would break, oh but hold on. Change is coming. Don't ever give up. Philippians 2:13 says, *"For it is God who works in you to will and to work according to His good purpose."* Philippians 1:6 says, *"He who has begun a good work in you will carry it on to completion until the day of Christ."*

I am convinced that one day we will get to the other side of the rainbow. I have my eye on the promise, and for now I will put a comma right here, until I turn the page of this chapter in my life. Stay strong. Know that if God brought us through all these tests and trials, He can and will bring you through too. Until then, you will find me holding up the Blood-Stained Banner. Now it is your turn. Will you grab onto the other side of the blood-stained banner as we hold it up together and lift one another up? The Bible says, *Two are better than one* (Ecclesiastes 4:9-12). Two are better than one, because they have a good reward for their labor.

Not Over Yet

Chapter 17

LESSONS LEARNED

There are so many lessons to be learned through all of this, so let me try to help you out with a few. It just may prevent you from having to go through something horrific like this.

I taught my son spiritual warfare but never taught him how to bind up the retaliation or to beware of the counterattacks. In spiritual warfare you must know the devil, your enemy. When you yield to the Lord and allow Him to use you to destroy the devil's kingdom, look out for a counterattack. There was a major battle going on for my son's heart and mind. Notice after Jesus was baptized, when He yielded to God's call upon his life, He immediately came under attack. We see the demon's counterattack during Jesus' time in the wilderness in Luke 4:1-2: *"Jesus, full of the Holy Spirit, left the Jordan and was led by the Spirit into the wilderness, where for forty days he was tempted by the devil. He ate nothing during those days, and at the end of them he was hungry."* Jesus was ready for the counterattack because He had fasted and prayed and stood on the Word of God. Rebellion opens the door for the devil to come in and have his way.

Remember, rebellion is as the sin of witchcraft (1 Samuel 15:23). Parents, don't fear man when they tell you how to discipline your children. Proverbs 23:13-14: *"Do not withhold discipline from your child; if you punish them with the rod, they will not die. Punish them with the rod and save them from death."* In 1 Samuel 3:13, God rebuked Eli for not disciplining his sons.

Just remember, when disciplining your children, never break their spirit. We have so many wounded adults from word curses that were spoken over them by a parent. Here are some examples that could have lasting effects: "Can't you do anything right?" "Why can't you be more like your sister?" "Stop being such a big baby." "I regret the day I had you."

The next thing is to be mindful of the company you or your children are keeping. Not only did God warn us that bad company would corrupt good character, but in 1 John 4:1 we are warned, *"Beloved, believe not every spirit, but test the spirit by the spirits whether they are of God: because many false prophets are gone into the world."* If your child says the friend is a Christian and their family goes to church, don't take them at their word. Don't let your emotions cloud your discernment. In this present age, evil still threatens those who belong to Christ. Just as people will play on your emotions, the devil will do the same to keep you distracted while he wreaks havoc. The Bible says in James 1:5, *"If any of you lacks wisdom, you should ask God, who gives generously to all without reproach, and it will be given to him."*

Please take heed to this next piece of advice: DON'T BAIL YOUR KIDS OUT EVERY TIME THEY GET IN TROUBLE. A LITTLE TOUGH LOVE WON'T HURT THEM BUT IT WILL SAVE THEM. Be careful that you are not in denial about what you are seeing or what is being told to you about your children. You will do them, yourself, and the community a disservice. Allow them to build their own relationship with Christ so when the battles come, they know how to fight.

Lastly, don't wait until it is too late to deal with the issues and get them counseling. Pay attention to their words and actions early.

Lessons Learned

Chapter 18

THE POEM

Daniel wrote the following poem to me from Juvenile Hall when he was 15 years old. I wish I had paid attention then, because I would have broken the curse and seen where the devil was working in him to silence and destroy him.

When I See Myself in the Mirror

When I see myself in the mirror
I look and smile
Contemplate for a minute
And think how I was raised as a child.

When I see myself in the mirror
I think back on how most people did me
Like violence was the remedy
And because I think of that
How I pray for my enemies
Not because of what I'll do
But because they don't know something better after here

The Poem

But everybody won't go.

When I see myself in the mirror
I sometimes get real sad
Contemplate again for a second
Thinking where in the hell is my dad.

When I see myself in the mirror
I see a scared little boy
That no one wanted to play with
Like an old broken toy.

When I see myself in the mirror
I see a boy suffering from social anxiety
Also wondering why the pain hurts so much inside of
me.

When I see myself in the mirror
I see a kid who has looked the wrong way
Done some wrong things
Who has kept a bad attitude
But that's what wrong brings.

When I see myself in the mirror

When I see myself in the mirror

Tears fall free from my eyes
I often look up to the sky and ask "God" why.
When I see myself in the mirror
I wish it would all just come to an end
Asking God's forgiveness
Because I'm tired of living a life of sin.

Looking back now on this poem, I can see how the devil was wanting to isolate him, destroy his self-esteem, label him, give him a poor self-image, and get him to feel unloved, abandoned, and rejected by God, his family, and society. Previously, I said I wish I had known about generational curses. I could have saved my children and myself a lot of heartache.

What are generational curses? They are curses passed down through actions of our parents, and our parents' parents (see Exodus 20:5, 34:7). My children's father had, from his dad, a generational curse of anger, rage, and abandonment. Ironically, Vance's dad was a police officer, but his son acted out in lawlessness, and spent time in many juvenile halls and camps, because of disobedience, truancy, stealing, and being affiliated with gangs. All of this was when he was 15 years old, prior to my meeting him.

Can you see the repetitive pattern with Daniel? Those spirits tried to attach to Solomon when he was a teen and into his early twenties. He found himself having a hard time controlling his temper. But Hallelujah! Glory to God! He broke the curse on his bloodline by wanting to be the total opposite of his dad. To this day, he is a great hands-on father, provider, and is even tempered!

The devil is relentless with those generational curses if you don't break them. If he can't get one generation, he will go after the next. So, the devil went after Daniel even harder with these generational curses. The devil waits and watches.

Remember the spirit of murder that came upon me when I found out their dad was cheating? That spirit also needed to be broken. That was a generational curse, and just like I obtained the knife to attack the mistress, a knife was now turned on me by my son. I raised the knife; my son actually used the knife. You see how the devil will escalate it from generation to generation if you don't break it. Pray and ask God to reveal to you what generational curses are in your family so you and your bloodline can be free.

Remember, the blood is enough. Hold up that blood-stained banner! Stand in the authority that Christ has given you. Tell your testimony. It will help you overcome the devil.

Remember, count the cost. God says if we suffer with Him, we will also reign with Him (2 Timothy 2:12).

The Poem

AUTHOR'S BIOGRAPHICAL SKETCH

Pastor Tanya Price is a native of Southern California, born in Hollywood. Tanya grew up in the city of La Puente, California, in a family of five girls and one boy. She is a licensed and ordained minister and co-pastors Precise Christian Ministries alongside her husband, Pastor Deno Price, in keeping with 1 Timothy 2:3-4. Pastor Tanya is a wife, mother of two sons, two stepsons, one grandson, and three granddaughters.

Pastor Tanya was not brought up in the church but somehow, as a little girl, she knew there was a God who loved her. Pastor Tanya recognized at the early age of 5 that the Lord was speaking to her through dreams and visons. She accepted Jesus Christ as her Lord and Savior at the age of 13 at a small Baptist Church in La Puente, California. At the age of 16, Tanya was filled with the power of the Holy Ghost with evidence of speaking in other tongues at Jesus Center in Inglewood, California, under Pastor Millwea Brooks Jr.

Pastor Tanya has supported and served many ministries as well as in the juvenile hall system. She realized in her late 20's that God had given her a powerful anointing to prophesy, bringing forth healing and deliverance. Pastor Tanya serves as the director of Royal Diadem Women's Ministry and also Beauty for Ashes Healing Ministry for men and women. She has been trained in spiritual warfare for deliverance ministry, counseling, prison ministry, prayer, intercession, and outreach to the homeless. God has put a burden on her heart for hurting women and single mothers. Pastor Tanya is an early childhood educator, and has taught as a preschool teacher, kindergarten teacher, and as a director for various preschools and afterschool programs.

She and her husband, Pastor Deno, were blessed to have owned and operated Precise Christian Academy in Philips Ranch, California. She loves to worship the Lord and ministers through liturgical dance. Pastor Tanya is on a mission to reach a lost and dying world for Christ! She is available for conferences, retreats, workshops, and ministry engagements.

***

Following are remarks from several of Pastor Tanya's family members and colleagues:

I have been blessed with the opportunity to have Tanya as my beautiful wife for 22 years. We have had our ups and downs but through it all she has always stayed faithful. As a mother to our blended family, she has been a blessing in giving our four sons guidance and encouragement, and teaching them to always trust and walk with the Lord. As a minister, she has been steadfast, committed, humble, and diligent in the Lord's work and, as we all know, her work is not done. I pray that this book will encourage you to stay faithful to the Lord and know that He can navigate you through any obstacles, tests, trials, pain, and suffering, through the power of His blood. This is evident in this book and in her life.

Pastor Deno Price
Senior Pastor, Precise Christian Ministries

About the author: I'm a firm believer that God, as well as the devil, knows exactly how our lives will play out from beginning to end. Like the military, both sides display their arsenal. At the point of my mother's conception, the devil began his counter assault. In hindsight, I see the powerful weapon of God that my mother has evolved to become. I now understand the many attempts by the devil to end her life. I also understand why God allowed it. He needed her iron sharpened. He needed the devil to know that her shield was made stronger than most. My mother is a survivor, and I am proud of her. Just like a caterpillar that has to go through complete metamorphosis to become a butterfly, Tanya Brodie became that butterfly as I watched. Though most know her as Tanya Price, I know her as Mommy.

I love you, Mom
Your oldest son, Solomon

About the author, my mother, Tanya Price, a strong woman of God!

The Lord blessed me with an amazing mother who is always there for me. When I was a child, my mother was a single parent who raised two boys. At times, we couldn't afford food or simple things in life like toys, clothes, etc. But my mom used to get down on her knees and pray to the Almighty God, and He heard her prayers and brought us through every situation. With that being said, that taught me that He will never leave us nor forsake us in life.

I love you, Mom
Your son, Daniel

What can I say about the author, Pastor Tanya Price, which hasn't already been said? She is a mother, a wife, a grandmother, a sister, an aunt, a student, a teacher, and many other wonderful things. But most importantly, she is a teacher, pastor, prophet, apostle, and daughter of the Most High God.

Pastor Tanya has always been many things to me, and I consider her my pastor, my mother, and my friend. She has successfully led, taught, and managed a daycare and church, and has done many other amazing things throughout her life. Through the process, she has also gone through numerous struggles, battles, and betrayals but she has always trusted and known the LORD our GOD would deliver her through all of them.

Pastor Tanya is also one of the most genuine and caring persons I know. She has a heart to worship God and intercede for others without thought. Because of this, there is no one more qualified to write a book on their life's story. I believe that this book you are holding will minister to your heart in a mighty way. It will help guide you through your struggles and give you hope that there is an all-powerful, all-knowing God in heaven who loves you and sent His Son to show that love through His sacrifice and redemption. This book will not only show you that God is watching over you, but that He is always attentive to your needs, and He will always deliver you from your trials and tribulations. I believe you are holding a gem in your hands, and I know the wisdom contained within these pages will share her triumphant turnarounds and victories. May God get all the glory out of this. Stay hopeful, blessed, and encouraged as you embark on this amazing God-glorifying journey.

Pastor David Munoz
Precise Christian Ministries

What can I say about the author and her work? I met Tanya over 25 years ago at Friendship Baptist Church in Yorba Linda, California. Although I observed her unique style of worship and crying before the Lord for weeks, we actually met and became friends through a mutual friend. When you saw one of us, you saw all three. We participated together in all night prayers, Saturday morning prayer gatherings, slumber parties, and women's conferences. Any events that focused on prayer, worship, and healing and deliverance, we were there. This behavior went on for years with the three of us.

Additionally, I remember often harassing Tanya to pray for me. That is, until one day she said, "You have the same power and access to God that I have." Now, why did she say that to me? She ignited a belief and ability to pray that was buried deep within me, but I did not comprehend the depth of the power and access of which she spoke. Nonetheless, it was history after that, and my life has never been the same. Moreover, there were many other incidents of correction and encouragement from Tanya that changed me, and subsequently, changed my life by propelling me into ministry.

We were all struggling, single parents, and even though I had employment at the time, my financial situation was the worst because I was also attending undergraduate school. On more than one occasion, Tanya blessed me with funds from her welfare check and never expected the money to be returned. Tanya is also partly responsible for the fact that I too serve in ministry in various roles.

Tanya, through the guidance of the Holy Spirit, helped and continues to help numerous men, women, and children to confront and heal from past trauma, both similar to and different from her own story. Also, Tanya has guided many nonbelievers to accept Jesus Christ as their Lord and Savior, to turn their lives around, and to embrace their various callings into ministry. She is a teacher of teachers.

Tanya has definitely lived this work. In some of her battles, I had a first-hand account of her faith in action, perseverance, trust, and her walk with God, as a testament of His transforming power. This was her journey to healing in order to birth the writings in this amazing book. She did not attempt to make the journey look effortless, but she never lost her trust in God. Tanya's testimony is real and raw, and I know it will encourage the broken to healing and the bound to freedom. Let her work speak to you, your heart, and the deepest hurt to serve as a catalyst to your own transformation. This book was written for you to know that God can do exceedingly above all that you can ask or think.

Tanya loves God and her family, friends, and congregation. She loves serving in ministry, helping others, and witnessing others living out their life purpose and calling. She is many in one — servant, worshipper, intercessor, teacher, and friend. I am honored to have the opportunity to write this testimonial, and most importantly, I am proud to call her friend. I know this work will be a blessing to many across the globe.

Dr. Alkenia Blackmon, MS, PPS/SC, Psy.D

Pastor Tanya Price, a licensed and ordained minister at Precise Christian Ministries in Upland, California, has been married for 22 years and is an educator, mother, and grandmother. She has been in the ministry of Jesus Christ for 29 years. She walks with a great anointing in teaching with wisdom and truth. Pastor Tanya Price operates in the gifts of God's Kingdom through the leading of the Holy Spirit for the deliverance of others through Jesus Christ our Lord. She gives Him all the glory.

She has written her testimony to share her life experiences with transparency, in the hope that through these tragedies and triumphs, you will see the great love of our heavenly Father over her life. Hopefully, you will be able to relate to her path to redemption through Jesus Christ.

We pray that her story will help you with your own choices as you walk in your path to deliverance, healing, victory, and ultimately, glory through Jesus Christ our Lord and Savior. Amen.

Pastor Javier Jimenez
Precise Christian Ministries

Like Jeremiah, the prophet of old, was called of God to be a chosen vessel unto the Kingdom of God, Pastor Tanya Price is a devoted woman of pure faith and moves in the divine gifts of the Spirit. I have witnessed many miracles and miraculous unexplainable things in her ministry. Through powerful prophetic teachings and spiritual prayers and healings, she has helped and reshaped many lives, including mine.

Pastor Tanya Price has spiritual and supernatural insight and foresight that's perpetually outstanding and profound. She is a devoted wife, leader, and friend. She has brought many to birth by the power of the midwife anointing. In the past 23 years I've known her, she's never changed. She is a woman after the heart of God. I highly recommend this masterpiece. Read it and you shall spiritually live.

Pastor Obelia Ashley
The Redeemed Ministries

AUTHOR'S CONTACT INFORMATION

Connect with me on:

Facebook

https://www.facebook.com/tanya.price.1840

Instagram

Arnette Price

Or Mailing Address

Pastor Tanya Arnette Price

Precise Christian Ministries

P.O. Box 9579

Ontario, California 91762

Via Email

precise.christianministries@yahoo.com

bloodstains2bloodstained@gmail.com

Or By Phone

(909)414-5401

Author's Biographical Sketch

32622915R00104